Case Study
Research
for Business

Case Study
Research
for Business

Jillian Dawes Farquhar

Los Angeles | London | New Delhi
Singapore | Washington DC

SAGE Publications Ltd
1 Oliver's Yard
55 City Road
London EC1Y 1SP

SAGE Publications Inc.
2455 Teller Road
Thousand Oaks, California 91320

SAGE Publications India Pvt Ltd
B 1/I 1 Mohan Cooperative Industrial Area
Mathura Road
New Delhi 110 044

SAGE Publications Asia-Pacific Pte Ltd
3 Church Street
#10-04 Samsung Hub
Singapore 049483

Library of Congress Control Number: 2011935136

British Library Cataloguing in Publication data

A catalogue record for this book is available from the British Library

ISBN 978-1-84920-776-8
ISBN 978-1-84920-777-5 (pbk)

Typeset by C&M Digitals (P) Ltd, Chennai, India
Printed and bound by CPI Group (UK) Ltd, Croydon, CR0 4YY
Printed on paper from sustainable resources

Summary of Contents

Contents

About the Author

Jillian Dawes Farquhar is Professor of Marketing Strategy at the University of Bedfordshire and leads the doctoral programme in the Business School. She has held research positions at the universities of Oxford Brookes and Northampton. Her research interests include publications in customer convenience, relationship marketing and branding in journals such as the *Service Industries Journal, Journal of Strategic Marketing and Marketing Theory*. She has co-authored the second edition of the *Marketing of Financial Services* and is editor of the *International Journal of Bank Marketing*, reflecting a long-held interest in research into the marketing of financial services.

Her expertise in research methods has been honed from supervision and examination of numerous doctoral and master's students' dissertations and theses. She has developed a M.Res degree and also contributed to the launch of the DBA programme at Oxford Brookes University. All of this has confirmed her belief that a solid understanding of research methods is essential not only in academic development but also in strengthening student critical faculties, preparing them for professional lives where an appreciation of research methods plays an increasing role.

Dedicated to my daughters Gail and Faith and to my friend Jean Jensen.

Profound thanks are due to Professor Jenny Rowley, Dr Toni Hilton, Dr Julie Robson, Nicolette Michels, Dr Ross Brennan, Dr Petia Petrova, Robin Croft, Bjoern Asmussen, Dr Jackie Clarke and valued colleagues in marketing and business.

I would also like to thank my long-suffering research and master's students who have inspired this work and from whom I learn continuously.

Introduction

Why have I chosen to write a case study research methods book? That is a question that I have repeatedly asked myself as I have laboured through the writing of this book. The answer is deceptively simple – many students that I have supervised have wished to pursue case study research and there was a need for a text to guide them. With due acknowledgement to the work that is already published in the area, I concluded rather rashly that perhaps I could write that guide, which would take the form of a straightforward text. This text would contain advice about how students could produce case study research that would satisfy readers and examiners. I was also aware, as an academic engaged in the teaching and assessing of research methods courses, that there were many assumptions about case study research which needed a forum for debate. Involvement over the years in the development and teaching of research methods on M.Res and DBA degrees, as well as supervising and examining doctoral students, might suggest that I had something to contribute, in particular to the credibility of case study research in marketing and business research.

This is not to suggest for one moment that there is an absence of exemplary texts on case study research. For example, Yin has written extensively about case study research but there did not seem one dedicated to students and researchers in business studies. Over several years of supporting business students in this type of research, it became evident that a text devoted to their specific needs was overdue. There is a unique interface between research and business where research rigour and practitioner value interact and this is something that this book attempts to address.

As I became more involved in reading the material on case study research across the disciplines, my plan turned into something of a mission. This mission was to play a role in strengthening the credibility of case study research in business, through encouraging and guiding researchers towards the submission of a coherent and consistent piece of research. I have been greatly assisted in this endeavour by some of the really wonderful research that is published and available for us all to learn from. Anybody writing a book has to dig deep into the subject area and I have learnt so much from the authors who have contributed to case study research and research methods more generally. Their intellect and endeavour are exemplary. I have also been aided by colleagues with whom I have worked in examining doctoral theses and co-supervising research students as well as my colleagues in the business and management research community.

Readership

Business and management students at a number of levels will find this book helpful. Undergraduate dissertation students, taught master's students and research students should all be able to extract valuable guidance about presenting an accomplished dissertation or thesis. Post-doctoral researchers who are new to case study research may also find that they can learn something from this text before moving on to more advanced works.

Aim of the book

The aim of the book is to provide a comprehensive but not an exhaustive guide to conducting case study research. It presents a framework for case study research onto which the researcher can append supporting arguments and detail about the steps in data collection and analysis. There are arguably two key components to a credible dissertation or thesis; first, developing a research strategy such as case study research and, second, paying relentless attention to detail. If these two components are convincingly addressed, then the reader/examiner should be favourably disposed to the arguments the researcher is trying to express. As with all research, there are some approaches that are hard to reconcile. For example, to those researchers who seek the answers to their questions based on generalizing from large samples, the idea of research that involves just a few cases is alien. Ontological divides in research are commonplace but this should not deter students from case study research. Like all research, it needs to be well executed and follow accepted protocols. It is just possible that some of the attacks on case study research may have arisen from studies that were not particularly well executed and that is something that reading this book can address. The mission also covered types of data. Case study investigation is quite commonly thought to consist of qualitative research but this is not the case. In the book, I suggest ways that quantitative data can form part of the data collection process. Case study research can also very valuably encompass at least secondary data, which is a disgracefully overlooked resource in some business disciplines.

Contents

This book is concerned with guiding readers in writing a dissertation or thesis following case study research methods. As case study research is a strategy, this activity necessarily involves using a variety of data collection and analysis techniques. Although overall guidance has been given about how these techniques fit with the strategy, detail about these techniques will need to be gleaned from texts dedicated to them. This book is, therefore, meant to be read in conjunction with specialist texts on research methods. I would expect my students to be studying a range of texts as a matter of course. It is part of their learning. Case study research is a strategy which encompasses a range of data collection and analysis methods, all of which need to be detailed and explained thoroughly. Evidence of reading and thinking needs to be provided at every key step in the research design.

Research does not happen in an orderly way but books about research do have to be structured in some way or other and this book is no different. It follows a path which is more or less similar to writing a dissertation or thesis, that is, there are sections on literature reviews, data collection and analysis. There are also chapters which address the nature of case study research, how case study research sits within research philosophy, case study research as a research strategy, research access and ethics, triangulation and a final chapter on writing up your research. Guidance is given on how data can be accessed, analysed, reported and presented so that they form part of a rigorously developed database, from which credible (yes, that word again) conclusions can be drawn.

Although most students usually start with a literature review as means of refining their research questions, they are usually engaged in doing a number of things at the same time. They can be revising sections at the same time as writing new ones, collecting and analysing data or developing new figures and tables. Readers will need to be aware that they will have to go back to rewrite sections in the light of new contributions to the area or some unexpected findings. The book attempts to recognize this recursive process whilst maintaining its logical structure. Whilst your relationship with your supervisors is vital in carrying out good research, the onus is on you to do the reading and thinking. Using this book to drive your strategy and inform the detail should assist you in submitting a robust piece of research based on case study research.

Good luck!

What is Case Study Research?

1

'Knowledge is power', Bacon (1561–1626)

Learning outcomes

At the end of this chapter, the reader will be able to:

- appreciate what case study research consists of and can achieve;
- provide basic arguments for the number of cases in a piece of research;
- understand the main criticisms of case study research;
- realize key ethical questions about case study research.

Introduction

In this chapter, we get acquainted with the basics of case study research as well as some basics of research more generally. All research is a mixture of fun, hard work and heartache, not necessarily in that order. You will learn as much about yourself as you do about your chosen topic, discovering new strengths as well perhaps as one or two unsuspected weaknesses. At this early stage, there are just two things that I would like you to bear in mind. First, there are no short cuts to good research. All the good students whom I have had the pleasure of supervising have worked very hard and I am afraid that the reverse is also true. Second, you have to be something of a 'completer-finisher' (Belbin 1981) in that you will have to persevere and address the detail as well as the strategy of your research.

You will also be dependent to a greater or lesser degree on a number of people or stakeholders in your environment. In the next section we discuss relationships in research.

Relationships in research

The most important person in your research is you and the outcome will depend on the work and the other attributes such as stamina, intellectual capacity and self-belief. A sustained project tests everyone's mettle. Although you are studying independently, that is you are not part of a structured work group and you are not being taught,

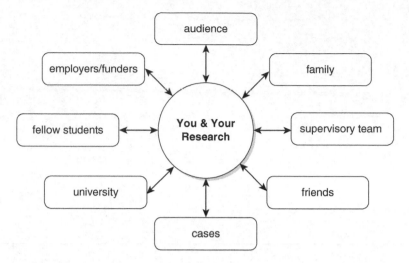

Figure 1.1   Stakeholders in your research

Adapted from Farquhar (2009)

you study within a framework of relationships with people who have a stake in your research. Figure 1.1 suggests who these stakeholders may be.

An obvious stakeholder is the supervisory team. Most research students have two supervisors these days who are academics with experience of supervision at your level and with knowledge of the area in which your investigation is based. You might like to confirm that this is the case. Your supervisors want you to complete your study successfully and to time. You will probably be allocated a supervisor in the first instance with expertise in the subject area and/or method. At doctoral level, it is essential that you have an experienced member of the team and at least one other team member who brings something relevant to the team, for example research expertise in a closely related area of investigation. You work as a team although you as the student produce the outcomes, that is, the chapters, presentations, conference papers or whatever has been agreed. Full-time study means just that – working as if you were carrying out a full-time job – a minimum of 35 hours a week (note the minimum). Since most academics work considerably more than that, do not expect any sympathy if you are not doing at least those hours. You will probably have some formal stages in your research progress that you will have to meet, for example registration and transfer from MPhil to PhD. Other targets will be more informal, for example submitting sections of your literature review and then draft chapters. You will agree dates with your supervisors. Supervisors will need to read these submissions before the next tutorial and will probably need them a few days in advance to do your work justice. Try to stick therefore to the agreed deadlines as your supervisors will have allocated time to reading your work. If you miss the deadline, then they will have plenty of other work to take its place. If your supervisors are not reading your work in advance of the tutorial and not preparing feedback, you are being disadvantaged and should seek formal redress. As a doctoral programme leader, I advise my colleagues that students should complete their theses in three years to a standard of minor revisions. Your supervisors will probably have this aim in mind too.

If you are studying part-time then your employers will have also have a stake in your research. The preferred scenario is that they fully support your studies in terms of time and payment of fees. This may not always be the case so you may wish to see if you can negotiate informally about some flexibility in your working commitments. Certainly get used to the idea of working weekends, holidays and late at night. That timetable brings us on to your family. A family stake can range from parents paying fees to being a partner but they may find it very difficult sometimes to understand what is involved and the strains of studying at a high and sustained level. Your friends can provide a very valuable function in offering you the social situations that you will need from time to time, so do not neglect them. The university has a significant stake in your research as well. The graduate school will provide training and support throughout your studies and you would be foolish not to fully exploit it. Most universities in the UK already have or are aiming to have a healthy research programme, which counts in a range of quality indicators, so they should be providing a good student experience. If they are not, you should complain. You will have fellow students who are also studying at your level. They will be researching similar or related topics and experiencing similar trials. Make the time to have a coffee with your colleagues at least once a week, as you will all gain from it.

Important stakeholders in your research are your cases, that is those organizations, teams, units or groups you choose to select and who consent to be your cases. We will talk in much greater depth about your relationships with your cases in Chapter 4. The final stakeholder is your audience who can be your supervisory team, your examiners, your readers, business and the academic community. The rest of this book will advise you how you can best relate to them through the writing and completion of your case study research.

Case study research?

One of the disconcerting aspects about research methods literature is that there is not always the agreement or consensus that a student might expect and this is certainly exemplified in case study research. It is important first to make a distinction between case studies that you may have encountered in teaching and case study research. This distinction is important as they are designed and written for quite different purposes. The case study that is used in teaching has been written as a means of training students for a career in business. It usually presents a real-life example of a company or organization and a specific example of some activity, usually discipline based. Questions are sometimes provided at the end of the case which aim to generate a class discussion. The students are supposed to bring their theoretical knowledge to the situation as a means of interpretation and/or recommending better practice. The analysis of the case consists of an application of theoretical understanding to a given situation. This kind of case is not the subject matter of this book as the role of theory is brought to a case. This book provides information about using a particular research strategy called case study research in order to respond to a research question and where data are gathered and analysed by the researcher. Case study research is usually defined as follows:

> A case study is an empirical inquiry that investigates a contemporary phenomenon in depth and within its real-life context, especially when the boundaries between phenomenon and context are not clearly evident.
>
> (Yin 2009: 18)

By using case study research, you will gain particular understanding or insight into whatever you have chosen to research which usually is a contemporary phenomenon. Case study research allows the researcher to look at the phenomenon in context. In business research, that means collecting evidence about that phenomenon where it is actually taking place, for example in a company, in a country or even in a university. In your case or cases, there is something that is of great interest to you and which you will argue will be of interest to others. In line with that view, Stake's (1995: 1) vision of case study research is that:

> we enter the scene with a sincere interest in learning how [actors] function in ordinary pursuits and milieus and with a willingness to put aside many presumptions while we learn.

Case study research is suitable for answering questions that start with how, who and why. Its further strength is that it is particularly well suited for investigating events that are occurring in a contemporary context; for example, you might be interested in how the takeover of Cadbury by Kraft is impacting on the career progression for graduate recruits. Case study research is concerned with investigating single or multiple units of study, using familiar research methods for data collection such as interviews or surveys. Case studies are empirical investigations, in that they are based on knowledge and experience, or more practically speaking involve the collection and analysis of data. By circumscribing the area of a study to a small number of units, the case study researcher is able to look in depth at a topic of interest or phenomenon. This small number of cases contrasts with large samples that feature in survey research. As such, case studies are preferred in the following situations (Yin 2009):

- When, how or why questions are being asked.
- When the researcher has little control over events.
- When the focus is on a contemporary phenomenon.

The research insight below illustrates research using case studies in retail banking.

Research insight: relationships in retail banking

Dibb and Meadows (2001) set out to investigate how relationship marketing was being applied in retail banking and chose four retail providers in the sector as units (or cases) of study in their research. The focus of the study was the application of relationship marketing, therefore the researchers were concerned about the current approaches and so had no control or influence at the time of data collection. Finally, the aim of the study was to capture how relationship marketing was being applied at that time so the phenomenon (relationship marketing) was contemporary.

Case study research is also concerned with studying the phenomenon in context, so that the findings generate insight into how the phenomenon actually occurs within a given situation. For business researchers, there are many advantages in looking at something within a particular location, company, team, department or industry. At the same time, these advantages have provided critics with ammunition about the wider contribution of these findings and which are discussed later in the chapter. The limitation of studying a small number of cases is that you will not be able to make statements about how your research can be extended to other situations as in survey research. This limitation is offset by the understanding that you gain an awareness of how this deep understanding can contribute to knowledge in business.

It is critical in case study research that you are very clear about the focus of your research and indeed this statement can be applied to all research. Creswell (2007: 73) describes a case as 'a bounded system' (for one case) or 'multiple bounded systems' (for more than one). What he means by bounded is that the researcher makes very clear statements in the research objectives about the focus and the extent of the research. Stake (1995) makes distinctions between different types of case studies. He states that an intrinsic case consists of a situation where you need to learn about a particular case, which could be a problem in a particular work situation. The second type of case, he argues, is an instrumental case, where you could use a case to learn about something else, for example the efficacy of cross-functional teams in managing customer relationships. Here you might choose any two teams within an organization which has relationships with its customers for the investigation. Finally, there is a collective case where you want to find out about a particular phenomenon from a number of different cases. An example of this type of case would be senior executive pay, where you might collect data from a number of organizations, for example banks and large retailers.

Because you are studying what seems to be a single case or a small number of cases, you may be lulled into thinking that it is easy to keep on track. A useful device of any research topic is to be able to tell people what your research is about in a single sentence. It is also very useful to keep this sentence and the research objectives in front of you when working as it may deter you from too much straying away from the track of your investigation. Research may evolve but if it does then the research objectives need to be revised and reframed, checking that the research topic is still focused and not in danger of getting out of control.

In responding to the questions of how, why and who in case study research, the essential tactic and a characteristic of case study research is to use several different sources of data within each case or cases (Yin 2009). Such data sources can include both primary and secondary data sources. In the Dibb and Meadows (2001) study, the sources of data consisted of internal documentation, industry reports (secondary) and two sets of interview data (primary). By using several different sources of data or different methods of data collection, the research findings are strengthened as the evidence is triangulated. Triangulation is an important concept in case study research because an investigation of the phenomenon from different perspectives provides robust foundations for the findings and supports arguments for its contribution to knowledge.

Case study research also enables a phenomenon to be studied over a period of time, that is, a longitudinal study. Longitudinal studies are not as common as they should be in business and management, and great insight can be gained by looking at a business phenomenon over a year or longer. An early example of case study research in business featured as part of the data in a three-year study of the transfer of new technologies from the developers to the users (Leonard-Barton 1990). The researcher argued that the close-up lens of the longitudinal study allowed the study of process and evolving patterns, which she was able to argue could be applied more widely to the transfer of new technologies.

What can case study research achieve?

Having arrived at a basic idea of what case study research is, it is now useful to understand what case study research can achieve. It has been described as having two outstanding strengths (Meredith 1998), both of which echo the definitions and views of the key contributors to case study research design:

- The phenomenon can be studied in its natural setting and meaningful, relevant theory generated from the understanding gained through actual practice.
- The case method allows the questions of why and how to be answered with a relatively full understanding of the nature and complexity of the complete phenomenon.

Case study research is ideal for looking at research questions which are closely connected to their context or situation, which in business is particularly appealing. Research questions of problems can be explored from perspectives that could be industry-specific, geographical location or size/type of business such as entrepreneurial or creative. Different functions such as accounting, operations or marketing can be investigated. For example, a study into working time regulations was conducted in the hospitality industry across two cases and uncovered the existence of accidental compliance with the regulations (Hurrell 2005). The first point refers to how theory can be generated from this understanding. Research is concerned with theory and how each study in some way contributes to theory in a given area. It is perhaps a weakness of the definitions cited earlier that neither mention theory when case study researchers go to great lengths to demonstrate how their research contributes to theory.

By understanding the capabilities and scope of a case study, the researcher will be able to develop the rest of the research. The aim of case study research is to dig deep, look for explanations and gain understanding of the phenomenon through multiple data sources and through this understanding extend or test theory. The value of case study research for business is that it allows the researcher to examine a problem or question in a practical, real-life situation. Readers of case studies expect a compelling argument for the choice of the case study research approach. For business, the advantages of this situational approach of case study research are significant. Case study research is particularly suitable for description, explanation and exploratory research or, as Yin (2009) suggests, case studies explain, describe, illustrate and enlighten. Stake (1995) argues that the real business of a case is particularization and understanding the case itself. Case study research is versatile in that the variety of data collection methods at the disposal of the case study researcher can be adapted to particular situations and conditions. In a larger organization, for example, it may be quite feasible to collect data using a survey of staff. Smaller organizations may lend themselves to a study of their documents and archives or in-depth interviews. As case study research usually involves a number of different data sources and methods, further insight is gained from considering the question from a multi-dimensional perspective. If there are multiple data sources, where does case study research fit in the research design? In this book it is argued that case study research is a research strategy, that is, it is the overall direction of the study upon which the rest of the research rests. Table 1.1 illustrates how case study research compares with other research strategies.

This comparison is useful in illustrating what case study research is not as well as what it is. Experiments and cases studies share the characteristics of a small number

Table 1.1 Comparison of case study research with experimental and survey approaches

Experiment	Case study	Survey
Small number of units	Small number of units (sometimes one)	Larger number of units
Data collected and analysed about small number of predetermined features of each unit	Data collected and analysed about large and often not predetermined features of each unit	Data collected and analysed about a small number of features of each case
Study of units organized in such a way as to control variables of interest	Interest in naturally occurring features or the variables in context	Units selected to represent characteristics of the study's population
Data usually quantified	Data can be quantitative, qualitative or both	Data usually quantified
Aim is of testing theory or evaluation of an intervention	Aim is to understand and theorize through enfolding the literature	Aim is to generalize findings from sample to population

Adapted from Gomm et al. (2000)

of units but they diverge in how the data are collected and analysed. Experiments are more concerned with relationships between variables, which are usually defined in advance. According to Collis and Hussey (2009), the aim in an experiment is to manipulate the effect of an independent variable on a dependent variable. For a survey, the aim is usually to measure key variables in a sample that represents a larger population and to generalize the findings of the survey to this larger population.

One or more than one?

As you will have seen above, the aim of case study research is not to make statements about the cases to a larger population but to explore in depth a particular phenomenon in a contemporary context. Nonetheless, an enduring question for researchers in case study research is how many units of study they should choose for their case study research. This question is not readily answered as it depends on a number of considerations which will be discussed more fully in Chapter 3. For the time being the following research insight is an example of the process one student went through in finalizing the number of cases.

Research insight: how many?

Frederick wanted to study tourism from the perspective of authenticity. The key question was how best to study the phenomenon of authenticity in tourism. He considered a number of possible cases to study this question. For quite some time, the study was going to consist of two units. Eventually Frederick settled on the single unit of South Africa so that he could illuminate the unique features of the case and how the research question could be addressed through this particular case.

The pressing question then is what might constitute a case or more properly unit of study? In business, a unit of study could be an individual, an organization, an event or an activity. If you wanted to investigate leadership, you may want to look at a particular individual or individuals and provide an analysis of leadership styles. If you were going to conduct a study into organizational culture, you would probably want to gain access to an organization (profit-making, charity, local government) and look in depth into that organization, study two departments of groups within that organization or make comparisons between two or more different organizations. You may want to evaluate, for example, the sponsorship of the London Olympics, where you might analyse how particular campaigns supported the marketing communications of a large beverage company. You may be seeking to find an instance of good practice which may involve looking at a number of units within a single organization. Cases, therefore, constitute a range of phenomena but the aim is to provide a rich multidimensional holistic picture of the situation (Remenyi et al. 1998) in a real-life context. Some examples of units of study in business research have included hospitality organizations (Hurrell 2005), process modelling projects (Bandara et al. 2005) and an urban university medical centre (Kaplan and Duchon 1988). The question of one or more than one unit of study is not easily resolved and the justification of the final choice needs to be carefully argued by the researcher.

Prejudice against case study research

If you understand some of the prejudice that case study research encounters, you will be able to construct and frame your research in such a way that your 'story' is credible. If your work is presented according to recognized and accepted research protocol, then reviewers or examiners will be largely satisfied.

Criticisms of case study research occur at three levels. The prime criticism levelled at case study research is that it lacks objectivity and rigour (Remenyi et al. 1998). Objectivity refers to the idea that reality is singular and separate or apart from the researcher. Objective research usually consists of experiments and surveys, where there is some distance between the researcher and the units of study. Although case studies may incorporate a survey, the aim of case study research is, as has been stated, an in-depth understanding of a contemporary phenomenon in context, therefore objectivity is not something that it is seeking to achieve. Indeed the case study researcher is often immersed in the case or cases and so the research can be described as subjective. Rigour is a term which arises constantly in research but its exact meaning is elusive. The view adopted in this book is that rigour can be achieved through a consistent and coherent research design, where the philosophical approach is stated at the beginning, an appropriate research strategy is adopted, data collection and analysis follow research methods, and protocols and justification for each phase of the research are provided.

At the second level of criticism, researchers who prefer quantitative studies, for example those experiments and surveys mentioned above, find the lack of large sample sizes of case study research disconcerting. They will worry about the lack of generalizability, as they know it, of the case study contribution. It is central to case study research to remember that the case itself does not constitute a sample of one (Bryman and Bell 2003) and that the aim of case study research is not to generalize the findings of a sample to a population. The issue of generalizability in case study research is a complex one and is presented in Chapter 7.

Finally, many of the criticisms levelled at case study research are also levelled at qualitative investigations. Some critics do not appreciate that case study research is not necessarily an example of qualitative research. Again, the responses to these criticisms should be addressed through the statement of clear research objectives, rigorous research methods and analysis and a transparent discussion of the findings. There are qualitative researchers who argue that this is playing the quantitative 'game' but it is hard to see how any of the above can be deemed a betrayal of qualitative research. As argued above, case study research is a strategy and as such the methods that are used for data collection can be qualitative, quantitative or incorporate both types.

As a research supervisor, one of the (many) things that I stress to my poor long-suffering students is that your dissertation or thesis must have a spine. By this I mean a strong thread that runs throughout the length of the investigation onto which everything that you discuss hangs. In a doctoral thesis which can be 100,000 words long, it is vital that the reader is reminded at regular intervals about the theme of the research and the consistency of the research method adopted. You should be able to map onto this spine every activity that you have conducted. This process will not be linear in spite of the metaphor of the spine. Some things will be re-visited, re-worked and re-interpreted but that should not stop you from carrying out this valuable activity. Arguably, this spinal map is even more important in case study research where the multiplicity of sources, data sets, analyses and findings make things a little more complicated than a study using survey research.

Ethical research

If you are researching as a student, it is very likely that your research proposal will be subject to ethics approval and that you will be provided with a set of criteria that it must meet. The following research insight is an example from a university's research guidelines.

Research insight: ethical research

Researchers are responsible for ensuring the following:

- Integrity – that the research has been carried out in a rigorous and professional manner.
- Plagiarism – that proper acknowledgement has been given regarding the origin of data and ideas.
- Conflicts of interest – that any financial or professional conflicts of interest have been properly declared.
- Data handling – that there has been effective record keeping, proper storage with regards to confidentiality and data protection.
- Ethical procedures – that proper consideration has been given to these and appropriate approval sought; should conform to professional codes of conduct where appropriate.
- Effective management and supervision of staff for whom they are responsible.
- Health and safety – that proper training has been provided and assessment of health and safety issues has been undertaken and appropriate action identified.

(www.beds.ac.uk/research)

The governing principle of research ethics can be reduced to 'do no harm', either to the research participants or to the wider world of research and the community of researchers. The case study researcher will become fully immersed in the context of the research, which may provoke some tension, and a thorough awareness of ethical research guidelines such as the above may assist in avoiding some uncomfortable issues.

Examples

You will do an immense amount of reading for your dissertation or thesis which will include different types of publications. You will be accessing reports, for example, I have been looking at UK government reports recently, research methods books, such as Yin (2009) or Creswell (2007), newspapers and practitioner publications, blogs, tweets and journal papers. All these publications have particular qualities, such as content, writing style, presentation, credibility and relevance to your research. Look at the style as well as the content.

Summary

It is worth remembering that the real business of case study research, according to Creswell (2007), is understanding the case or cases themselves through an interpretation of the data. Case study research is exciting, although arguably all research is exciting, and has a great deal of potential in business research which is only slowly being acknowledged. However, its role will only be fully appreciated if research in this tradition is well executed. This is the challenge owing to the range and variety of methods available to case study researchers, so the onus is very much on the researcher to present their work in such a way that it overcomes the prejudices that exist.

- Independent study might require a different mindset to your previous learning experiences.
- Case study research is concerned with investigating a unit of study or multiple units of study using familiar research methods such as interviews or surveys.
- Case study research is suitable for providing a holistic in-depth investigation into a contemporary phenomenon in a particular context.
- Criticisms of case study research can be addressed through clear statements of the research objectives, adherence to accepted research protocols and transparent research methods.
- Ethical research practice is as important in case study research as anywhere else with particular attention to 'do no harm'.

Exercises

1 Explain what case study research is and the type of research questions for which it is well suited.

2 Outline when it may be appropriate to use single or multiple case studies.
3 Outline the discussion of the benefits and weaknesses of case study research.
4 Describe key ethical issues arising from case study research.

Key words

Relationships: you are not alone in your research and you are part of a network. Take the time to find out how to make the most of this network.

Prejudice: researchers are a mixed bunch and have their own preferences and views. In some disciplines, case study research is not particularly well received; if you are doing case study research, you have an obligation to do it well and perhaps change some minds.

Further reading

Maylor, H. and Blackmon, K. (2005) *Researching Business and Management*, Basingstoke: Palgrave Macmillan.
Remenyi, D., Williams, B., Money, A. and Swartz, E. (1998) *Doing Research in Business and Management: An Introduction to Process and Method*, London: Sage Publications.
Yin, R. (2009) *Case Study Research: Design and Methods*, fourth edition, Thousand Oaks, CA: Sage Publications.

References

Bandara, W., Gable, G. and Rosemann, M. (2005) 'Factors and measures of business process modelling: model building through a multiple case study', *European Journal of Information Systems*, 14, 347–360.
Belbin, R. (1981) *Management Teams: Why They Succeed or Fail*, London: Butterworth-Heinemann.
Bryman, A. and Bell, E. (2003) *Business Research Methods*, Oxford: Oxford University Press.
Collis, J, and Hussey R. (2009) *Business Research*, third edition, Basingstoke: Palgrave Macmillan.
Creswell, J. W. (2007) *Qualitative Enquiry and Research Design: Choosing Among Five Approaches*, Thousand Oaks, CA: Sage Publications.
Dibb, S. and Meadows, M. (2001) 'The application of a relationship marketing perspective in retail banking', *Service Industries Journal*, 21, 1, 169–194.
Farquhar, J. (2009) 'Stakeholder branding in financial services', *Proceedings of the 4th International Conference on Services Management*, Oxford.
Gomm, R. Hammersley, M. and Foster, P. (2000) Introduction, in R. Gomm, M. Hammersley and P. Foster (eds), *Case Study Method*, London: Sage Publications.
Hurrell, S. (2005) 'Dilute to taste? The impact of working time regulations in the hospitality industry', *Employee Relations*, 27, 5, 532–546.
Kaplan, B. and Duchon, D. (1988) 'Combining qualitative and quantitative methods in information systems research: a case study', *MIS Quarterly*, 12, 4, 571–586.
Leonard-Barton, D. (1990) 'A dual methodology for case studies: synergistic use of longitudinal single site with replicated multiple sites', *Organizational Change*, 1, 3, 248–266.

Meredith, J. (1998) 'Building operations management theory through case and field research', *Journal of Operations Management*, 11, 3, 239–256.

Remenyi, D., Williams, B., Money, A. and Swartz, E. (1998) *Doing Research in Business and Management: An Introduction to Process and Method*, London: Sage Publications.

Stake, R. (1995) *The Art of Case Study Research*, Thousand Oaks, CA: Sage Publications.

Yin, R. (2009) *Case Study Research: Design and Methods*, fourth edition, Thousand Oaks, CA: Sage Publications.

Philosophical Assumptions of Case Study Research

2

Learning outcomes

At the end of this chapter, the reader will be able to:

- understand the importance of research philosophy in conducting case study research;
- develop arguments in support of research philosophy in a case study investigation;
- appreciate the role of research paradigms in case study research;
- appreciate the distinction between deductive and inductive research and how they relate to case study research;
- respect that case study research should not violate accepted research approaches.

Introduction

Researchers often become engrossed in the detail of their research, such as the statistical techniques they are using for their questionnaire data, the precise approach for their sampling or the coding of their interview data. Whilst the importance of detail in research is fully accepted, ultimately the credibility of your research rests on the philosophical assumptions that underpin your research. These assumptions do not just form a bolt-on section at the beginning of your dissertation or thesis but drive all the arguments that you develop, the language that you use, as well as the data collection/analysis. It is interesting to note that the major contributors to case study research understanding (Stake 1995; Yin 2009) actually come to this research strategy with rather different philosophical assumptions about case studies, demonstrating the flexibility of the strategy. This flexibility in the assumptions of case study research is, at the same time, a strength and a weakness. It is a strength in that case study research can be used as a strategy in diverse contexts and to address a range of research questions. The flexibility can be a weakness in the way that the research is executed, where it may be misinterpreted as a lack of rigour by readers. In this chapter, the research philosophies that underpin case study research and how these philosophies inform the whole of the research process will be explored and discussed.

Research traditions

It is tempting at the beginning of your research to get immersed straight away in the detail of research methods such as data collection, data sources and refining the questions that you are going to ask. Whilst all of these activities are indeed very important, the foundations of your research also need to be embedded in the early stages of your study. These foundations will be shaped by the philosophical assumptions that your investigation rests upon. The starting place for this philosophical contemplation is how you, the researcher, see the world and the view that you have of reality. This may sound rather profound but we do not all see the world in the same way. You will know about divergent views from the discussions you have had with family, friends and even strangers! If you stop to think about it, differing views of the world pervade our lives and affect the way that we formulate our arguments, the way that we interpret evidence and hence the way that we will ultimately conduct and present our research. The following insight follows the well-trodden path of the differing perspectives that people may have on particular phrases that occur in day-to-day language.

Research insight: Calm down, dear!

A row in the UK House of Commons erupted in 2011 over the Prime Minister's use of the phrase 'Calm down, dear' to a female member of the opposition. The phrase that the PM used was a key line in an advertising campaign by a large motor insurance company, where the star in the advertisement urged female drivers to calm down. The PM was accused of being deeply patronizing for using this comment. The star of the advert, when interviewed, responded to this outcry by describing it as an example of the lunacy of political correctness and said that he thought the people involved lacked a sense of humour.

Is the citing of this phrase an example of an offensive remark or is the furore that followed an example of extreme political correctness? I asked a group of friends at the time and there was a pretty even but irreconcilable split.

In this book, the discussion of research philosophies begins with an overview of the two broad approaches proposed by Kuhn (1971). Kuhn described these two approaches as paradigms, which offer students a philosophical framework for shaping their research. Each paradigm comprises an accepted set of theories and methods, which researchers tend to follow as they give the research coherence. It is this word 'accepted' which is of importance to the budding researcher who is learning about research and how to conduct their own investigation. For your research to have the coherence that the reader/examiner is looking for, you will need to demonstrate that you have a good understanding of the research protocols which are consistent with the research paradigms. The reader/examiner will want to be reassured that you are conversant with these protocols and expect to see evidence that you have followed them in your research.

Within the two research paradigms proposed by Kuhn (1971), there are three key areas that will drive the researcher's overall research approach. First, every researcher will have an ontological stance, that is, the way that they view the world. This stance is nomothetic if they assume that reality exists independently or objectively as a structure, which is distinct from individuals' perceptions. Conversely, if the researcher believes that the world is socially constructed and understood only by examining the perceptions of participants or actors, then their ontology is ideographic. The ontological assumptions of the researcher then lead to ideas about the way in which they understand how knowledge is derived and what knowledge is valid. The study of knowledge – in particular, the nature, sources and limits of knowledge – is referred to as epistemology.

Epistemology is concerned with the sort of knowledge that such-and-such is true, for example that the world is a sphere. It is not concerned with other forms of knowledge, such as knowledge of how to cook. It may be helpful to consider a central question in epistemology, which is: what must be added to beliefs to convert them into knowledge (Klein 1998, 2005)? It is unlikely therefore that you would be writing the word 'believe' in your study, as you need to be more interested in how that belief can be substantiated through research. For researchers whose ontology is nomothetic, their epistemology is usually positivist. A positivist believes that phenomena are real and precise (e.g. measurable) and, as a consequence, will adopt a research design that allows them to measure what they are investigating. For researchers, who favour a closer engagement with the research phenomenon, their epistemology is interpretivist, phenomenological (Remenyi et al. 1998) or social constructionist (Easterby-Smith et al. 2008). There are a number of different terms that encompass research that falls under the heading of the ideographic ontology rather confusingly, so you need to make sure that you are quite clear, or as clear as you can be, about the particular epistemology that you are embracing for your research. In this book, non-positivist traditions will be referred to as interpretivist. Interpretivism is predicated on the belief that the social world requires a different logic, which reflects the distinctiveness of humans (Bryman 2001).

The researcher has now thought about their ontology and the epistemology that is derived from that ontology. Additionally, the researcher will need to appreciate the values that will drive their studies and this is referred to as axiology. Axiological assumptions again vary according to the researcher's ontology. The positivist researcher, whose ontology is nomothetic, will broadly subscribe to the view that science and the process of research is value-free, and that they are quite detached from their observations. This researcher is concerned with eliminating bias at every stage of the study. The interpretivist researcher, on the other hand, believes that values help determine what are considered to be facts and the interpretations that are drawn from these facts. The interpretivist researcher acknowledges that their research may indeed have bias but insists that this is a feature which they explain and address.

In more practical terms, research is frequently referred to as quantitative or qualitative. Originally, these terms referred to the nature of the data in research, for example quantitative data are generally data that have been acquired through some form of measurement. These terms have gradually come to mean more than just ways of collecting data. Quantitative research, as opposed to quantitative data, is often a consequence of following the positivist tradition. Qualitative research is, on the other hand, more consistent with the interpretivist approach. These descriptions are simplifications and, as you become familiar with the literature, you will note the nuances that writers have attached to the usage of these terms. Although research is not confined to positivist and interpretivist epistemologies and the paradigms in which they are embedded, they do tend to prevail in research and business research, in particular. These two dominant epistemologies are now explored in greater depth with specific reference to case study research.

Positivism

Positivism recognizes the centrality of theory. It revolves around discovering patterns in observable events and describing them in the form of laws, with an emphasis on identifying causal relationships and providing explanations. The positivist researcher seeks knowledge phenomena on the basis of measuring and observing (Collis and Hussey 2009). As a consequence, they often develop and test hypotheses, following what is referred to as hypothetico-deductive methods. In hypothetico-deductive research, a theoretical statement is formulated, for example from a review of the literature. The statement is then broken down into a set of hypotheses which are then tested. The testing often involves the measurement of variables and the researcher is looking for evidence to refute the hypothesis. In Chapter 5, positivist methods that are appropriate for case study research are described and explained. Although initially this epistemological approach seems quite straightforward, closer examination of positivism reveals that it is notoriously difficult to pin down. Fortunately for the researcher, there are some elements which are common to this epistemological approach (Bryman 2001), as shown in Table 2.1.

Some of these elements may sound familiar to you. This familiarity is not surprising given the dominance of positivism in how people think that knowledge can be gained. Observation is at the core of the positivist's approach to research, as in some of the natural sciences. The business researcher, however, very quickly runs into constructs such as leadership or consumer wants which are less easy to observe. How to observe and measure the unobservable aspects of the social world are key pre-occupations for the researcher with positivist inclinations. As a consequence, positivist researchers will

Table 2.1   Elements of positivism

Element	Description
Observation	Only knowledge confirmed by the senses can be warranted as knowledge and as such is verifiable.
Operationalization	Concepts need to be operationalized so that they can be measured.
Hypothesis generation	The purpose of theory is to generate hypotheses which are then tested to allow for explanations.
Objectivity	Science is value-free.
Independence	The researcher needs to be independent from that which is being observed.
Causality	The aim of science is to find causal explanations and fundamental laws that explain regularities in human behaviour.
Generalizability	In order to explain regularities in behaviour, it is necessary to select samples of sufficient size from which inferences can be drawn about a wider population.
Reductionism	Problems as a whole are best understood if they are reduced to the simplest elements.

Compiled from Bryman (2001), Easterby-Smith et al. (2008) and Lee and Lings (2008)

expend a great deal of effort on how to operationalize these unobservable concepts to enable the data to be collected. Hypotheses that form the basis for observations of these concepts are usually generated from relevant theory. The axiological stance of the positivist researcher is value-free, that is they aim to remove bias from their research at every stage and strives to be as independent as possible from what is being observed. Causality is concerned with cause and effect and the aim is to find out if A caused B. Experimentation is the method best suited to discovering the relationship between a dependent and independent variable where the aim is to try to hold everything else constant. Generalizability refers to whether the findings of a piece of research can be transferred to other situations. An example of generalizability would be whether your investigation about consumer buying practices in UK supermarkets can be extended to European consumers. Generalizability, or the lack of it, is a common criticism levelled at case study research and indeed at interpretive research. The response to this criticism is that the purpose of the research is not to make statements about a population but instead to examine a research phenomenon in context and in depth. Reductionism, which is the final element in the table, aims to simplify research so that control of the experiment or investigation is maintained and a good understanding of how the variables under investigation are behaving is gained.

As positivism is an epistemological approach that has been 'borrowed' from the natural sciences by social sciences and business, it is concerned with knowing about natural objects and discovering the laws that apply in this natural world. The prime objection, therefore, to positivism is that it fails to take account of the social world, which is constructed through meanings and 'the practices predicated on them' (Hughes 1980: 123). The observations that a positivist researcher makes may therefore be fallible as they may not lead to a full understanding of any social situation. Within the business literature, it has been argued that positivism ignores dynamism (Buttle 1998) and is unable to predict the more complex outcomes of networks and relationships (Easton 1995), such as those that exist in business. Given these criticisms of the positivist orthodoxy, the discussion moves on to consider the other paradigm that Kuhn (1971) called interpretivism.

Interpretivism

Interpretivist traditions are concerned with grasping individual and unique truths with an emphasis on understanding or *verstehen*, as described by Weber (1947). These traditions, which can include phenomenology (Remenyi et al. 1998), hermeneutics and social constructionism (Easterby-Smith et al. 2008), are based on the belief that humans interpret the world that they inhabit and attribute meanings to this world. Interpretivism acknowledges the subjective meanings used in social interaction. The researcher is not a detached observer, as suggested by positivism, but an active agent in the construction of the world through the specific ideas and themes incorporated in the relevant form of knowledge. Complete objectivity is not the aim in interpretivist research and, in fact, interpretivists argue that it is valuable to be able to gain an understanding of cultural realities. Instead of the distance of the positivist researcher in minimizing bias, the interpretivist researcher seeks to be neutral and to achieve transparency in their research (O'Leary 2004). Thus, a distinguishing characteristic of interpretivism is the centrality of the interaction between the investigator and the object of investigation, as it is only through this interaction that deeper meaning can be uncovered. The researcher and their participants jointly create or co-construct findings from their interactive dialogue and interpretation (Ponterotto 2005). One of the principal challenges that an interpretivist

Table 2.2   The characteristics of interpretivist research

Element	Description
Understanding	Reality is viewed as socially and societally embedded and exists within the mind. It is fluid and changing and multiple realities are presumed.
Subjectivity	This involves interpreting the meanings and actions of actors according to their own subjective frame of reference.
Subjective	Knowledge is constructed and based on shared signs and symbols recognized by members of a culture. Research encompasses researchers' own views and how they have been constructed.
Setting	The emphasis is on natural settings, and the subject of research is not removed from what surrounds it in everyday life. It involves an in-depth investigation.
Holistic	To interpret a phenomenon, the researcher must look at its parts in terms of its whole and the whole in terms of its parts.
Rich insight	By exploring in depth, the researcher can gain a much fuller understanding of the phenomenon.

Compiled from Creswell (2007), Gribich (2007) and Lee and Lings (2008)

researcher faces is the lack of definition between the different methodologies (Goulding 1998). These characteristics are summarized in Table 2.2.

Nonetheless, there are common characteristics of this approach. Samples, if you even want to use that term and some interpretivist researchers do not, tend to be small and non-probabilistic. Interviewing is often described as 'in-depth' with questions designed to encourage informants to talk freely. The role of the researcher can even be that of participant. They openly acknowledge bias and position themselves in the research to interpret the data from their own experiences (Creswell 2007). Interpretivist researchers tend to relish complexity and avoid the reductionism that characterizes positivist research.

It can be seen from the overview of the dominant paradigms that each one has its limitations. Positivist research can claim to be scientific and researchers of this orthodoxy can present their findings quantitatively. In many fields, numbers and statistics have an authority that carries, at times, unwarranted weight. Objectivity and detachment also imply rigour and methodological soundness without necessarily delivering it. If the researcher is left unimpressed by the scientific detachment of positivism, then there are considerable attractions to be found in the interpretivist camp, where subjectivity, involvement and closeness are not only acceptable, but encouraged. Researchers are not necessarily restricted to being unequivocally positivists or interpretivists, as there is some flexibility within the research paradigms.

Critical realism

To address some of the challenges arising from the positivist paradigm in business research, a school of thought known as post-positivism has emerged. Both positivism and post-positivism share the goal of an explanation that leads to the prediction and control of phenomena. Both perspectives emphasize cause–effect linkages of phenomena that can be studied, identified and generalized. Both approaches proffer an objective, detached (Ponterotto 2005) and deterministic researcher role based on a priori theories (Creswell 2007).

The emphasis in post-positivism falls on following specific procedures to ensure that the observations gleaned in the research are verifiable, accurate and consistent. Within the post-positivist stable sits realism. Realism resembles positivism in that it is theory-driven but realism does not make the clear separation between theory and observation that the positivists do. For realists, all data are theory-dependent.

Although realism has its adherents in business research, for example Shelby Hunt (1990), a version of realism known as critical realism is attracting attention from case study adherents (for example, Easton 2010). Advocates of critical realism believe that there is a reality independent of our thinking that science can study but, importantly, they acknowledge that observation is fallible. The critical realist agrees that our knowledge of reality is a result of social conditioning and, thus, cannot be understood independently of the social actors involved in the knowledge-derivation process (Dobson 2002). However, it does take issue with the belief that the reality itself is a product of this knowledge-derivation process. Easton (2010) has recently argued that critical realism has considerable value to case study researchers as it mirrors the language and procedures that we routinely adopt and the explanations that we create. The critical realist, within a business context in particular, accepts that our world is socially constructed but not entirely so, as reality makes an appearance. Sayer (2000: 17) explains this point more fully:

> Critical realism acknowledges that social phenomena are intrinsically meaningful and hence the meaning is not only externally descriptive of them but constitutive of them (though of course there are usually material constituents too). Meaning has to be understood, it cannot be measured or counted, and hence there is always an interpretative or hermeneutic element in social science.

This extract demonstrates the fusion of some of the positivist and interpretivist thinking, which is generally good news for the business case study researcher in that it allows for flexibility in the research approach. It makes a conscious compromise between extreme positions by recognizing social conditions (e.g. class) as having consequences whether they are labelled or observed but also recognizes that concepts are human constructions (Easterby-Smith et al. 2008). For the critical realist, not everything has to be amenable to observation, as theory is 'allowed' to make an appearance in providing explanations (Bryman 2001). Critical realism has three basic contentions:

1   The reality to which scientific theories primarily aim to refer is the structures and mechanisms of the world rather than empirical events. Structures are defined as sets of internally related objects and mechanisms as ways of acting. Objects are internally linked in a structure in the sense that their identity depends on their relationship with the other components of the structure, for example the employer–employee relations itself presupposes the existence of employment contracts etc.
2   The underlying structures and mechanisms are only contingently related to empirical events.
3   Although scientific knowledge of reality is never infallible, it is still possible to acquire knowledge through creative construction and critical testing of theories (Tsang and Kwang 1999).

The case study researcher, in adopting a critical realist approach to their case study investigation, could be concerned with the causal relationship between key entities.

Critical realism allows generalization to theory of the entities involved, the ways in which they interact and the nature of the mechanisms through which they interact (Easton 2010). Case study researchers have further choice in their epistemological foundations for their study, which includes mixed methods research.

Mixed methods

The increasing acceptance that a combination of approaches yields considerable advantages (e.g. Bryman 2001), recognizes that a more rounded and richer picture of social phenomena can be generated through a mix of methods. Attached to mixed methods is the question that the researcher must consider of incommensurability. Incommensurability refers to the fundamental paradigmatic distinctions between positivist and interpretivist approaches to research. It can be argued that the two dominant research traditions are fundamentally irreconcilable as they represent opposing ontological assumptions. For researchers, the vital question is whether research in business and management can be conducted from multiple philosophical paradigms (Lee and Lings 2008). The short answer is 'no', it cannot. The subjectivity of interpretive research and the objectivity of positivism cannot be brought together in any coherent or convincing way – they are ontologically and epistemologically incompatible.

Nonetheless, it is increasingly being recognized that the mixed methods approach offers significant benefits to research. Mixed methods refer to the ways that data are collected and analysed. It is quite common for a research project to involve interviews and a survey but there should be a dominant research philosophy guiding the overall study which will influence the research objectives and the type of contribution that the study makes. This view is consistent with the critical realists, as we have seen, but is also being advocated by pragmatist researchers. Pragmatists argue that the two-paradigm view expounded by Kuhn is too narrow in the pursuit of knowledge (Morgan 2007). Table 2.3 proposes how the pragmatic approach differs from the traditional two-paradigm approach that has dominated the discussion so far.

In this table, three dimensions of research are presented, first the connection in research between theory and data. Induction and deduction are discussed in the next section with abduction. The relationship to the research process within the paradigmatic approach is described here as intersubjective. Intersubjectivity refers to a state in between objectivity as preferred by the positivists and the subjectivity of the interpretivists. Often attached to intersubjectivity is 'common sense', so that social actors live and experience life without necessarily questioning the meaningful structure of the world. We make sense of our actions and those of others through a 'stock of knowledge' that is held in common and that we inherit and learn through members of society (Hughes and Sharrock 1990: 138). In a pragmatic approach, therefore, there is no problem with asserting both that there is a single 'real world' and that all individuals have their own unique interpretations of that world (Morgan 2007).

Table 2.3 A pragmatic alternative to the key issues in social science research methodology

Research dimensions	Interpretive	Positivist	Pragmatic approach
Connection of theory and data	Induction	Deduction	Abduction
Relationship to research process	Subjectivity	Objectivity	Intersubjectivity
Inference from data	Context	Generality	Transferability

Adapted from Morgan (2007)

For case study researchers, mixed methods research can present a very attractive option and many of the published case study research papers involve sets of qualitative and quantitative data as the following research insight illustrates. This more flexible approach to case study research has been exemplified by Eisenhardt (1989) and Eisenhardt and Graebner (2007), who are significant contributors to case study literature. The following research insight drawn from the work of other case study researchers provides an example of mixed methods research in a case study.

Research insight: frustration at first

Kaplan and Duchon (1988), in their longitudinal investigation into the interrelationships between perceptions of work and a computer information system, collected data via interviews, participant observation (qualitative) and from a questionnaire using a Likert-style response format (quantitative). Each data source was analysed with the quantitative data yielding 'nothing reportable'. A return to the qualitative data suggested that the staff formed two groups with different orientations to their jobs. This interpretation of the data led to a re-analysis of the quantitative data which this time indicated significant differences between the two staff groups.

It is worth reiterating that mixed methods do not constitute a research philosophy—the term merely describes a mix of methods which in themselves should form part of the study's epistemological stance. It is quite likely that you, as a researcher, will use a range of methods in your case study research but doctoral students certainly will be expected to have developed an epistemological foundation for their enquiry.

Table 2.4 provides a concluding overview of the key distinctions between positivism and interpretivism, so that you can give a quick preliminary check that your

Table 2.4   Concluding implications of Kuhn's paradigms for case study research

	Positivism	**Interpretivism**
Researcher	Detached	Engaged
Research question	What	Why, How
Values	Free	Laden
Concepts	Clearly defined to enable measurement	Defined but open to reconsideration during course of research
Units of analysis	Classified and simplified	Rich in themselves and complex
Generalization underlying logic role of theory	Deduction Theory testing through hypothesis formulation, data collection and testing	Induction Generation of theory through pattern analysis
Samples	Random	Selected according to research objectives
Finding	Measure	Meaning

Adapted from Maylor and Blackmon (2005) and Easterby-Smith et al. (2008)

planned approach does not violate accepted research assumptions. You can then begin to think about alternative approaches that have been discussed above.

Do return to the contents of this table as your research progresses, so that your research maintains the consistency that will mark it out as a coherent and rigorously conducted investigation.

Research logic

An important consideration in creating the foundations of your research is whether you are taking a deductive or inductive approach. Rather than adding to the philosophical demands of research, if you understand the difference between these two approaches of logic, you will be able to maintain the coherence of your work. Knowing the shape that your research should take should lessen the risk of making mistakes in its structure and overall integrity.

Deductive research (see Figure 2.1) is where a theory or conceptual framework is developed and then tested (Collis and Hussey 2009), or where you move from a general law to a conclusion about a specific instance. This research logic follows a structured process that often starts with a conceptual framework that explains behaviour or a social phenomenon that you are interested in studying (Maylor and Blackmon 2005).

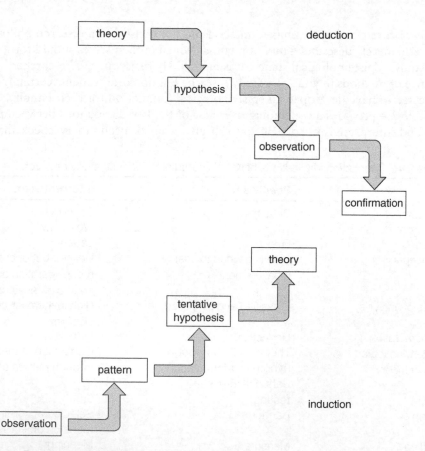

Figure 2.1   Deduction and induction

You then go on to test this framework within a particular area. If you are using the word 'test' in your research objectives, then you are probably taking a deductive approach to your investigation. It may also follow that you are going to collect quantitative data, say, via a survey (Maylor and Blackmon 2005). Deductive research is often summarized as theory testing, usually with a sample where the findings of the research may be generalized to a population. The following research insight provides guidance into deductive case study research.

Research insight: confirmatory cases

Johnston et al. (1999) argue for case study research in testing theory. They state that case study research must begin with theory where hypotheses could, for example, propose the presence of a phenomenon under certain conditions. They then assert that the research design must be rigorous, specifically the definition of the unit of analysis, the selection of appropriate and multiple cases, which data to collect and how to collect it. They believe that independent evaluation of the findings may address some of the criticisms that are levelled at case study research.

Inductive research is possibly slightly more common in case study research. Here, the aim of the researcher is to generate theory from the data, by looking for patterns in the data (Maylor and Blackmon 2005). Inductive research is, therefore, concerned with exploration and understanding – aims consistent with case study research. The research question is framed in terms of the importance of the phenomenon and the lack of plausible existing theory (Eisenhardt and Graebner 2007).

As Lee and Lings (2008) point out, in research, the distinctions between the two styles of logical reasoning will not always be easy to disentangle. A combination of both styles is, therefore, not unheard of, as the following research insight demonstrates.

Research insight: technology trust

In a study of two connected cases (Cisco and Compaq), existing theory on inter-organizational trust was extended to explain a process framework on how trust can be used to contribute to perceived benefits, organizational performance and B2B e-commerce success. Ratnasingam (2005) argued that establishing trust in the underlying technology infrastructure had become an important driver for value realization. The author collected both quantitative and qualitative data in her study from primary and secondary data sources and mapped her findings across four perspectives of trust-technological, economic, behavioural and organizational. The research extends previous literature on trust to explain a process framework within the context of B2B e-commerce. The study is characteristic of much research in that it follows neither inductive nor deductive reasoning exclusively, although the research is guided by a firm conceptual framework.

The pragmatic approach to research is to rely on a version of abductive reasoning that moves back and forth between induction and deduction, thereby recognizing the limitations of a purely inductive or deductive approach to reasoning. Abduction is the development of an explanatory or theoretical idea, which results from close examination of particular cases (Hammersley 2005). Hammersley (2005) goes on to state that this process of inference is not a matter of logic, either deductive or inductive logic, but instead, according to Thomas (2011), it is making a judgement which offers the best explanation for the observations that you are making.

Once more, the message is that research needs to be consistent with accepted research protocols derived from an understanding of research paradigms and logic.

Case study research and philosophical assumptions

What do the preceding discussions signify for the student embarking on case study research? As will be argued throughout this book, case study research is a strategy, but like any research strategy, it will be influenced by the researcher's assumptions about the world that they inhabit and how they perceive knowledge. Case studies tend to follow an inductive reasoning in that they tend to build theory rather than test it. If your research is leaning towards the inductive approach, then Eisenhardt (1989) provides a very thorough overview of the process of building theory from case study research (see Table 2.5).

There are many ideas in this table which you may not yet be familiar with. Each step in the left-hand column has been labelled with the chapter in the book where these ideas are discussed.

However, there are researchers who pursue a deductive approach to case study research and the research insight into confirmatory cases is just such an illustration (Johnston et al. 1999). More recently, Bitekine (2008) has proposed theory testing using qualitative data in case study research. This researcher borrows a case study design from medicine (prospective) where the hypotheses are formulated a priori so that they are tested consistent with deductive logic. He argues that the 'rich data from a live social process' (p. 177) can generate important insights into the explanatory power of theories. Deductive case study research is less common than inductive or abductive investigation but provides another approach to the capabilities and opportunities that case study research offers.

Summary

This chapter has sought to enlighten you about the philosophies that underpin research in general and yours in particular. Your research will be more convincing to the reader and you will be able to argue for the contribution of your research more effectively if you understand these underpinnings:

- Assumptions that case study research is largely interpretivist, inductive and qualitative, are unfounded.

Table 2.5   The process of building theory from case study research

Step	Activity	Reason
Getting started (Ch. 3)	Definition of research question	Focuses effort
	Possibly pre-determined constructs	Provides better grounding of construct measure
	Neither theory nor hypotheses	Retains theoretical flexibility
Selecting cases (Ch. 3)	Specified population	Constrains variation and sharpens external validity
	Theoretical, not random, sampling (Ch. 3)	Focuses effort on cases that extend theory
Crafting instruments and protocols (Ch. 5)	Multiple data collection methods (Ch. 5)	Strengthens grounding of theory by triangulation of evidence
	Qualitative and quantitative data combined	Gives a synergistic view of evidence
Entering the field (Ch. 6)	Overlap data collection and analysis, including field notes	Speeds up analysis and reveals helpful adjustments to data collection
	Flexible and opportunistic data collection	Allows investigation to take advantage of emergent themes and unique case features
Analysing data (Ch. 6)	Within-case analysis	Gains familiarity with data and preliminary theory generation
	Cross-case pattern search using divergent techniques	Forces investigator to look beyond initial impressions and see evidence through multiple lenses
Shaping findings (Ch. 7)	Iterative tabulation of evidence for each construct	Sharpens construct definition, validity and measurability
	Search for evidence of 'why' behind relationships	Builds internal validity
Enfolding the literature (Ch. 7)	Comparison with conflicting literature	Builds internal validity, raises theoretical level and sharpens construct definition
	Comparison with similar literature	Sharpens generalizability, improves construct definition and raises theoretical level

Adapted from Eisenhardt (1989)

- The choice of research tradition drives the whole of the research strategy, including phrasing of research objectives, data collection and data analysis and detail.
- Research logic can intermingle but you should know whether you are working towards theory testing or theory developing.
- Case study research can combine methods but not research traditions, owing to an incommensurability of paradigms. Nonetheless, a third approach of pragmatism is acknowledged.

Exercises

1 Using the Association of Business School's journal grading list (or equivalent), identify a grade four journal in your discipline that you can access. How many articles in this journal are written according to a positivist epistemology? What characteristics of a positivist epistemology can you identify?
2 Using the same journal, see how many case studies you can find as a research strategy. Note down three arguments that the authors have used to justify their case study approach. If there are no case studies, move on to another journal.
3 What are the implications of understanding the research paradigms for the credibility of case study research?

Key words

Paradigm refers to a set of beliefs that leads to a particular research approach, such as scientific, and influences within that approach how research should be done.

Ontology is the theory of social entities, for example subjective.

Epistemology is the theory of knowledge and is usually driven by the researcher's ontological view.

Further reading

Easterby-Smith, M., Thorpe, R. and Jackson, P. (2008) *Management Research* (3rd edition), London: Sage Publications.
Eisenhardt, K. (1989) 'Building theories from case study research', *Academy of Management Review*, 14, 4, 532–550.
Remenyi, D., Williams, B., Money, A. and Swartz, E. (1998) *Doing Research in Business and Management: An Introduction to Process and Method*, London: Sage Publications.
Thomas, G. (2011) *How to do Your Case Study: A Guide for Students and Researchers*, London: Sage Publications.

References

Bitekine, A. (2008) 'Prospective case study design: qualitative method for deductive theory testing', *Organizational Research Methods*, 11, 1, 160–180.
Bryman, A. (2001) *Social Research Methods*, New York: Oxford University Press.
Buttle, F. (1998) 'Rules theory: understanding the social construction of consumer behaviour', *Journal of Marketing Management*, 14, 63–94.
Collis, J. and Hussey, R. (2009) *Business Research*, third edition, Basingstoke: Palgrave Macmillan.
Creswell, J. W. (2007) *Qualitative Enquiry and Research Design: Choosing Among Five Approaches*, Thousand Oaks, CA: Sage Publications.
Dobson, P. J. (2002) 'Critical realism and information systems research: why bother with philosophy?', *Information Research*, 7, 2. Available at: http://informationr.net/ir/7-2/paper124.html
Easterby-Smith, M., Thorpe, R. and Jackson, P. (2008) *Management Research* (3rd edition), London: Sage Publications.

Easton, G. (1995) 'Comments on Wensley's *A Critical Review of Marketing: Market Networks and Interfirm Relationships'*, *British Journal of Management*, 6, S83–86.

Easton, G. (2010) 'Critical realism in case study research', *Industrial Marketing Management*, 39, 1, 118–128.

Eisenhardt, K. (1989) 'Building theories from case study research', *Academy of Management Review*, 14, 4, 532–550.

Eisenhardt, K. and Graebner, M. (2007) 'Theory building from cases: opportunities and challenges', *Academy of Management Journal*, 50, 1, 25–32.

Goulding, C. (1998) 'Grounded theory: the missing methodology on the interpretivist agenda', *Qualitative Market Research: An International Journal*, 1, 1, 50–57.

Gribich, C. (2007) *Qualitative Data Analysis: An Introduction*, London: Sage Publications.

Hammersley, M. (2005) Assessing Quality in Qualitative Research. Paper presented to ESRC TLRP seminar series: Quality in Educational Research, University of Birmingham, 7 July. Available at: www.education.bham.ac.uk/research/seminars1/esrc_4/index.shtml (accessed 29 April 2011).

Hughes, J. (1980) *The Philosophy of Social Research*, London: Longman.

Hughes, J. and Sharrock, W. (1990) *The Philosophy of Social Research* (3rd edition), Harlow: Pearson.

Hunt, S. D. (1990) 'Truth in marketing theory and research', *Journal of Marketing*, 54, 1–15.

Kaplan, B. and Duchon, D. (1988) 'Combining qualitative and quantitative methods in information systems research: a case study', *MIS Quarterly*, 12, 4, 571–586.

Klein, P. (1998, 2005) 'Epistemology', in E. Craig (ed.), *Routledge Encyclopedia of Philosophy*, London: Routledge.

Kuhn, T. (1971) *The Structure of Scientific Revolutions* (2nd edition), Chicago: University of Chicago Press.

Lee, N. and Lings, I. (2008) *Doing Business Research: A Guide to Theory and Practice*, London: Sage Publications.

Johnston, W., Leach, M. and Liu, A. (1999) 'Theory testing using case studies in business-to-business research', *Industrial Marketing Management*, 28, 201–213.

Maylor, H. and Blackmon, K. (2005) *Researching Business and Management*, Basingstoke: Palgrave Macmillan.

Morgan, D. L. (2007) 'Paradigms lost and pragmatism regained', *Journal of Mixed Methods Research*, 1, 1, 48–76.

O'Leary, Z. (2004) *The Essential Guide to Doing Research*, London: Sage Publications.

Ponterotto, J. (2005) 'Qualitative research in counseling psychology: a primer on research paradigms and philosophy of science', *Journal of Counseling Psychology*, 52, 2, 126–136.

Ratnasingam, P. (2005) 'Trust in inter-organizational exchanges: a case study in business-to-business electronic commerce', *Decision Support Systems*, 39, 525–544.

Remenyi, D., Williams, B., Money, A. and Swartz, E. (1998) *Doing Research in Business and Management: An Introduction to Process and Method*, London: Sage Publications.

Sayer, A. (2000) *Realism and Social Science*, London: Sage Publications.

Stake, R. (1995) *The Art of Case Study Research*, Thousand Oaks, CA: Sage Publications.

Tsang, E. and Kwang, K.-K. (1999) 'Replication and theory development in organizational science: a critical realist perspective', *The Academy of Management Review*, 24, 4, 759–780.

Thomas, G. (2011) *How to do Your Case Study: A Guide for Students and Researchers*, London: Sage Publications.

Weber, M. (1947) *The Theory of Social and Economic Organization* (trans. A. M. Henderson and T. Parsons), New York: Free Press.

Yin, R. (2009) *Case Study Research: Design and Methods* (4th edition), Thousand Oaks, CA: Sage Publications.

Developing Your Case Study Research Strategy

3

Learning outcomes

At the end of this chapter, the reader will be able to:

- provide a rationale for case study research as a research strategy for the investigation;
- appreciate the need for a strong conceptual framework;
- articulate the arguments for the number and types of cases chosen;
- outline the role of triangulation in case study research.

Introduction

Good research is achieved by having a consistent research design where methods and overall direction are presented logically and coherently. The starting place for a coherent dissertation or thesis is the formulation of research objectives. Once the research objectives have been formulated, then the strategy for achieving the objectives can be worked out. The stance adopted in this book is that case study research is a research *strategy*, that is, it provides the framework and overall direction of the research. From this overall direction, the detail of the research methods flows. In order for you to be able to argue for case study research, it is helpful to have insight into other strategies that may also be open to you for your research. You will need to read other research methods books and journal papers carefully and allow yourself time to think about the overall shape of your research and how the detail of the research fits that shape. All your thinking must be accompanied by reading, which will consist of subject-specific material, research methods literature and study guides. Your university will provide guidelines on your dissertation or thesis. Additionally, you are advised to consult publications which give valuable advice on how to complete a dissertation or thesis successfully. I always advise my research students to get hold of one of these books and insist that they read them regularly throughout the period of study.

This chapter is concerned with developing your research strategy following case study protocols. These protocols are not as straightforward as you might expect. As in all research, writers have their own views and ideas, so that there is not the consensus about case study research that a student might hope for. What follows is a distillation of much of the work in case study research and my own experience as a writer/supervisor.

Developing your research question and objectives

The idea of a strategy for your research may be new to you but you probably have thought about how you might get hold of the information as well as arriving at the topic that drives it. Many students think that a questionnaire, or more properly a survey, is going to suit their research. You will have conversations with your supervisor about your data collection at an early stage of your research and you will discuss a range of alternatives. It is important that you prepare for these meetings by reading the research methods literature in business and social sciences to get an overview of the options that are open to you. You need to achieve a 'fit' between what you want to accomplish and how you are going to accomplish it. This chapter will debate what case study research is particularly suited for.

You may be already thinking that case study research is the strategy that you want to pursue but before even thinking about your research strategy, you need to articulate your research question or problem. There is really no substitute for writing this down and even if you cannot manage a title just yet, make sure that you can capture your research in *one* sentence. This is an important exercise as it makes you think about the research question/problem clearly and to some extent puts you in charge of it. In this process, you become the 'owner' of the research and this is an important step in acquiring the mantle of a research student.

As you reflect and refine your research question and its objectives, ensure that you use the right sort of vocabulary. There are two dimensions to this. First, as discussed in the previous chapter, the research approaches express distinctive ontologies, therefore the research questions and processes that underpin them are going to be quite distinctive as well. Postivists and post-positivists such as critical realists will tend to use words that are consistent with theory testing, for example *hypotheses* or *to determine*. Interpretivists will use vocabulary that mirrors theory development such as *emerging* and *experience*. Establishing that you are familiar with the research methodologies at an early stage will set the tone of your dissertation or thesis.

This discipline about vocabulary should also be extended to your research topic, where absolute precision about your terminology needs to be maintained throughout your investigation. Your precision will reassure the reader that you have taken charge of your investigation and that you are completely familiar with the concepts that you are discussing. Take the time to think very hard about what you want to study, what you want to achieve and what it is likely that you will be able to achieve within the constraints of your situation. The constraints of your situation may be driven by the length of time available and the level of the research, that is, whether it is a taught master's or a full-time doctoral thesis. Essentially, the firmer the foundations of your research, the stronger your investigation!

In your reading of the literature relating to your research topic, you may think that you have identified a 'gap' in this literature, as the following research insight illustrates.

Research insight: impulse purchasing

Anja wanted to investigate impulse purchasing as an aspect of consumer behaviour in retailing. Her reading of the work in the area indicated that much of it had followed

(Continued)

(Continued)

a positivist epistemology and as such was quantitative and deductive. She thought and argued that an alternative approach could yield new insights. She created three research objectives that reflected this inductive approach that she thought would add to the theory in the area. After consultation with her supervisors, she chose a multiple case study strategy, where her data would be generated by a longitudinal study of ten cases of female German shoppers. Her work yielded new insights by showing impulse purchasing was often regarded as a positive experience by her informants, whereas the existing literature tended to suggest that the experience was negative.

As this research insight shows, there have been studies into the phenomenon of impulse buying which used a deductive approach where a theory was tested. This investigation, when completed, offered new insights that had emerged through using an inductive or theory-generating approach. Therefore, you can argue with reference not only to the literature itself but also to the research methods that an alternative research approach could yield new insights into the phenomenon. It is very likely that your research objectives will be modified somewhat during the course of your research, especially as you become more familiar with the literature in the area. This does not, however, in any way suggest that you should not go through the process of formulating objectives early in the research process. The following research insight demonstrates the process of refining research objectives.

Research insight: business-to-business relationships

Pei-Fang wanted to investigate how the take-over of a building society by a much larger organization was going to impact on the motivation of its sales team. Having identified a broad research question, she narrowed this down to a statement about an exploration into how the motivation of a sales team may be affected during the period of a take-over. The 'how' in the question suggested that a case study was a viable research strategy. Alternative strategies could also have included a study where in-depth interviewing formed the main data collection method. After discussions with her supervisors, she decided on a case study as she had been able to gain access, somewhat unusually in financial services, to two building societies experiencing similar sorts of change. Case study research was going to enable her to study the phenomenon of motivation within the context of take-over in building societies, a highly contemporary question after the credit crunch in financial services. Having made the decision about the research strategy, Pei-Fang could then move on to reading more about her selected research strategy, the literature on motivation and background information about financial services.

If you have not yet got to the stage of clearly formulated research objectives, Stake (1995) suggests that you write down a set of research questions (10–20) which you can gradually reduce to a more manageable two or three. Do not expect your supervisors to take too active a role in this process. The investigation is to be carried out and completed by you and therefore you need to 'own it'. You will 'own it' when

Table 3.1   Examples of wording of research objectives

Deductive	Inductive
Test	Explore
Determine	Discover
Identify	Uncover
Measure	Understand
Variables	Aspects

you have done the reading and the thinking (don't forget the thinking!) about the phenomenon and research methods. You are embarking on a period of independent learning where you are in charge of your own destiny. This may sound rather portentous but for doctoral students, it is a long journey into uncharted territory, where you will encounter all sorts of new experiences, not all of which will be pleasant. The upside is that you are learning all the time and will become a much sharper thinker with well-developed research skills. The phenomenon, therefore, *must* be of interest to you and you must also want to find some sort of answer to the question or problem that you pose.

Once you have arrived at a research question, it is then time to think about how you are going to tackle the work that this question sets. Breaking down the title into research objectives is the first step. I suggest to my students that they need to phrase the research objectives in line with the research approach that they are taking (see Table 3.1).

In doing this seemingly insignificant task, you are adding to the overall coherence of your research and sending a signal to your readers that you have grasped the epistemological arguments of your investigation. It will also focus you in those moments when you seem to lose track. The first objective could be about developing a conceptual framework for your study in which the literature review which will act as the theoretical background to your study. The second objective could refer to the research methodology or strategy that you will be deploying to achieve your research. You would say here if you were going to use a case study research strategy, for example. The final research objective should advise the reader of the outcome of the research. For doctoral students, this would be the contribution to knowledge or for master's students the implications of the research for theory and/or practice. Some students have more than three objectives but there is nothing to be gained by having more than about five. The title, working or not, and the research objectives should be written above your workspace so that you do not deviate too often down attractive but ultimately fruitless avenues.

Designing your research

Once you have got your research question/problem and research objectives to a 'working' stage, you then need to set out the shape of your research. Students usually find it helpful to structure their research on a chapter-by-chapter basis. Although the number of chapters can vary, most research studies rest on three legs – the conceptual framework, the research design and the discussion/contribution. These three legs form a tripod, which supports the whole dissertation or thesis (see Figure 3.1).

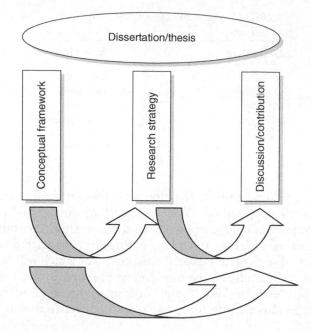

Figure 3.1   Research tripod

Each leg itself needs to be carefully constructed so it forms a solid foundation for it to feed into the overall research. This is one reason why you need to keep the research question/problem and objectives in front of you all the time, so that you can relate the contents of each leg back. Each leg is also interconnected to the other two legs. In the conceptual framework, you develop the theoretical basis for your investigation. This conceptual framework will lead into a rationale for your research strategy, for example multiple case studies. The discussion section of your research consists of a closely argued discourse of your findings and how these findings combine with the conceptual framework. It is more important that you map your work this way at this stage, rather than chapter by chapter, so that you have an overall view of the substance of your research. These tripod legs will be revisited throughout this book.

This tripod is the foundation for your research structure no matter how many chapters you plan or finish up with. Within the tripod, Yin (2009) suggests five components in the table overleaf (see Table 3.2) for a blueprint of case study research. These components will need to be included but actually where they appear will be resolved as you write your research. The research question can be restated several times, for example in the introduction, at the end of the literature review as a means of introducing the conceptual framework and again in the conclusion.

This table provides a preliminary overview of the components of a case study strategy and all of these components will be revisited in depth in later chapters.

Developing the conceptual framework for case study research

As argued in Chapter 2, case study research involves empirical method, which is described as a 'procedure employing controlled experience, observation or experiment

Table 3.2   Components of case study research design

Component	Case study
Research question	Use the literature to refine the research question. It is not necessary always to find a 'gap'. It may be quite sufficient to explore a phenomenon in a new context, use a different research design or revisit a question that has not been explored recently. With case study research, you are usually posing a 'how' or 'why' question.
Propositions/ objectives	You will develop a set of propositions or objectives that will direct you to study a particular aspect of the research question and how it may be studied, i.e. the source of data.
Unit of analysis	This relates to the basic problem of what the case is. What are the bounds of the case and what is the focus of the investigation? The research propositions need to define this. If the research question does not lead into the specification of a unit of analysis, then it may be too vague or broad. Make sure that you can explain clearly what the unit of analysis is to a colleague.
Linking data to propositions	This refers to the analysis of the data. If theory is driving the data collection and analysis (deductive), then the propositions structure the data and discussion. If data are generating theory (inductive) then structure tends to be based on emerging patterns.
Interpretation of findings	The literature will have debated rival theories and studies and you will return to these in interpreting your findings.

Adapted from Yin (2009)

to map out nature of reality' (Remenyi et al. 1998: 282). The collection of the evidence that forms the empirical method should not be collected without reference to underlying concepts. The empirical evidence which you do collect needs to be considered with reference to the conceptual framework or theoretical constructs that have guided its collection in the first place. In case study research, the role of theory, according to Yin (2009), is part of the blueprint structure. Yin is sometimes referred to as a positivist (Myers 2009) and it is consistent with this epistemological approach that theory is developed and tested. Whether you think you are a positivist, an interpretivist or a critical realist, theory forms one of the tripod 'legs' of case study research. The following research insight emphasizes the role of theory in case study research.

Research insight: business networks

In a study of business networks, Halinen and Törnroos (2005) discuss case study research as a strategy for theory development (i.e. inductive). They conclude that an underlying theoretical standpoint is essential in this style of research. The theory continues to guide the research through data collection and analysis. It then provides the necessary frame of reference when facing critical questions of whether the research has generated new insights or aspects into the theoretical domain.

Yin (2009) is at pains to point out that students need not be concerned with 'grand theory' but that it is important to have propositions (see Table 3.2). We shall talk about a framework rather than propositions but the principle is roughly the same.

The conceptual framework of your study will be constructed by means of a thorough and critical review of what has been written about your research topic or what is generally referred to as 'the literature'. From this literature, you will extract through reading and reflection the key concepts that relate to your research question. This process is often lengthy and challenging, both in terms of intellect and endurance. It comes at a time when you are learning how to do research and so often takes longer than you might think. When reading the literature, note how the authors present their conceptual frameworks both in words and images and which you will then construct to build your framework. The literature usually refers to the academic work that has been published, but you will need to read the range of sources listed below:

Books: reading the books in your discipline will allow you to begin to concentrate on the relatively narrow area that will form the foundation of your research question. Good research results from a thorough investigation of a relatively tightly constructed research area. Supervisors will reject research proposals that are too broad as they consider them too hard to complete within the timescales available as well as achieve the standard required.

Journal articles: these form the mainstay of your investigation. Once you have refined your topic sufficiently to a range of search terms, then you can start using the databases that your institution has access to. If your searches are not generating a reasonable number of hits, you are either being too specific or not using the right terms. If this is the case, then return to the books to check that you have grasped the key concepts of your chosen area. At this stage, you are exploring the theory that will inform your research. The context of your particular research may not be reflected in the theory.

Practitioner press: case study research is very concerned with the context of the investigation and so looking at the press that relates to the context of your case is important for your research.

Research insight: consumer confidence in food retailing

Eleanor was planning to investigate the consumption of juices and smoothies in families. She planned multiple case study research on a longitudinal basis in which she would investigate how families were coping with the economic downturn. As part of her research, she had been reading the food retailing press which suggested that the purchase of smoothies was an indicator of consumer confidence. At the same time, the costs of this product are strongly affected by rises in commodity prices. As a result of her reading, she chose smoothies as a proxy for luxury food spending.

(Based on www.thegrocer.co.uk/articles.aspx?page=articles&ID=216834)

Government, Federal and European data sources are very rich. For example, the author had recent recourse to Office of Fair Trading reports for a project. Further reading will include newspapers, online sources, magazines, digital media and TV and cinema which will provide essential background in understanding the research question and its context. Make friends with your institution's library staff. Most librarians have search skills that make the rest of us weep with envy. It is also worthwhile discussing the progress of your research with your other research colleagues. They may have been reading in similar areas or have acquired some insight into a related topic.

When you are reading all this material, make written notes of what you are reading rather than just highlighting. Although highlighting has its uses, writing things down encourages you to think about what you are noting down. In writing up the conceptual framework for your study, you will have to convey to the reader that you have reflected upon the theory, what the implications of this theory are for your research and how the literature is informing the development of this tight framework. The reader will be looking for a reflective and critical account of what has been written in the literature that you argue relates to the research question. You will only be able to convey this if you have gained a very firm grasp of the relevant work.

Do not overlook what other guidance you can obtain from what has been written in your chosen subject area. For example, you will gain valuable information about how experienced researchers developed their research design, the arguments that they used and how they analysed their findings. The literature also provides you with very good examples of how to present your data and which will be revisited in Chapter 6. The role of literature in your study is to specify the key constructs that underpin your research and it will also provide you with guidance on research methods. Reading and reviewing the literature on the research design adopted in the theoretical area that you are investigating will help you to provide a solid foundation for your study. The identification and absorption of key works in your subject area is an indispensable part of the learning process and cannot be short-circuited. The conceptual framework forms the basis for the analysis of the findings of your investigation as the tripod structure demonstrates (Figure 3.1). The following research insight illustrates how this happens.

Research insight: click-and-mortar e-commerce

Adelaar and his colleagues (2004) wanted to explore how customer value created by click-and-mortar e-commerce influenced the geographical market reach of retail outlets. The theoretical framework for their multiple case study research was developed and adapted from Ansoff's growth matrix. They replaced the original dimension of 'new markets' with a dimension of what they called 'geographical market reach'. The researchers discussed the findings of their cases with reference to that framework. The use of a theoretical framework in this investigation also enabled the researchers to delimit their research so that value was being interpreted specifically. This important step of drawing the boundaries of their research then directed the selection of units or cases, the data collection and analysis.

I usually suggest to my students at master's and doctoral level to present the framework of their research in a diagram (see, for example, Figure 3.2).

In this conceptual framework of international sports sponsorship, the author illustrates the overall logic behind sports sponsorship (resources and entertainment) as

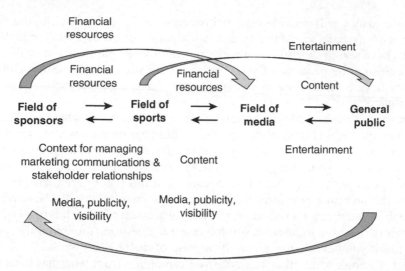

Figure 3.2   Example of a conceptual framework for international sports sponsorship

Adapted from Olkkonen (2001)

well as the actors (fields) that underpin the logic. The important activity here though is the mapping of the concepts and how they are associated with each other.

At master's level, a diagram of your conceptual framework does not need to be completely original. It is acceptable to adapt an existing model to convey your core research question and its components. At doctoral level though, an examiner would expect to see an original conceptual framework developed from the literature. It is then much easier to argue for the contribution that your work has made to knowledge in the area.

Case study: a research strategy

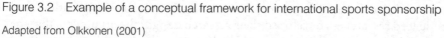

The conceptual framework that you have spent so much time and energy developing should lead into a discussion of the research strategy that you are adopting for your study. The reader will be looking for a convincing argument about the choice of a case to address the research question. To do this, you must be able to list what the case study approach will allow you to do, as argued earlier. Adopting a case study research strategy is particularly suitable for:

- In-depth investigations where you are generating intensive insight.
- Flexibility so that you can adapt your research to changes.
- Studying the research question in context.
- Investigating a complex research problem.

At this stage, you should revisit the draft of your research question and objectives to check whether they reflect these characteristics. As stated in Chapter 1, case study research is particularly suited for looking at a phenomenon *in depth* and *in context*. Unlike experiments where the variables are controlled, case study research does not attempt to control the context (Yin 2009). Case study research is apt for *exploring, explaining, understanding* and *describing* the research problem or question. You may want to check that your research objectives use this sort of vocabulary. You are not going to be able to make statements about the findings being applicable to a wider population but you are going to be able to provide in-depth perceptions or insight into a particular question and its context. If your reading about case study research leads you to believe that this strategy is going to provide an effective way of addressing your research question or problem, then the research objectives must reflect what case study research does best.

Your objectives should also specify the type of data that you intend to collect under the overall strategy of the case study. By choosing the epistemological stance of your case study strategy, you will follow a predominantly positivist or an interpretivist epistemology and accordingly generate, analyse and present those data consistent with these epistemologies. The strategy of case study research forms a backbone that runs the whole of your research enabling you to be consistent with what you are trying to achieve. Case study research can be embedded in any of the traditions described in the previous chapter. One of the strengths of case study research is that it can involve quantitative and qualitative data or a mixture of both but the data overall need to be aligned with the epistemological stance that your research is based on.

Creating the case study strategy

Just as in any other research design, the unit of analysis from which the data are generated forms a focal part of the research. As discussed in Chapter 2, classical positivist researchers are concerned with objective studies, where samples are investigated with a view to generalizing the research findings to a wider population. Indeed, many of the statistical techniques that they use require a sample of at least a hundred units. Consumer research, for example, often consists of a sample of consumers which are then broken down into categories of age and sex and a variable of interest, for example the length of a relationship that a customer has with a financial institution. Management research may involve smaller groups of informants, who are selected on the basis of them of having particular insight into the research question (see, for example, Lähdesmäki and Siltaoja 2010). In both of these examples, each of the units is a case in terms of research methods language. This could be rather confusing but the distinction is that in case study research, the unit of analysis is once more a case but the research is bounded by the case or cases themselves (Maylor and Blackmon 2005). This bounding comes about because there is something about the case or cases that is inherently interesting and that merits the case or cases to be studied in their own right (Stake 1995) rather than a means of collecting data as part of deductive or inductive research. Thus, the research question and the case are intertwined. This intertwining can make life rather challenging for the researcher, so this is where the clarity of the research objectives becomes imperative.

Choosing your case(s)

Your review of the literature will have suggested not only the conceptual framework for your research, but also the conditions under which a particular phenomenon is likely to be found or perhaps not found (Yin 2009). For example, looking at conflict in employee relations suggests finding an industry or organization where this conflict exists. Equally, there may be considerable advantage in accessing a case where there is a low level of conflict between management and staff. Through formulating clearly defined objectives from a thorough review of the literature, the number and types of cases can be argued convincingly. Once again, this point establishes the importance of building your work on the three legs of the tripod.

The procedure for the selection of cases is sometimes referred to as sampling. You will have come across this term before and it is indeed a staple of research but more commonly a process related to survey research. In case study research, you are not seeking to draw a sample from which you can generalize the findings to the population from which the sample is drawn. If you are thinking along those lines, then you might want to revisit your thinking about your research strategy. The rationale for selecting your cases is that they are particularly suitable for 'illuminating and extending the relationships of the constructs' (Eisenhardt and Graebner 2007: 27), which make up your conceptual framework. In other words, the selection of your case(s) is largely directed by your conceptual framework and is therefore purposive. There are some suggestions to help you though in this significant decision. Eisenhardt (1989) discusses theoretical sampling where the goal is to choose cases which are likely to replicate or extend emergent theory.

Practically, there may be some adjustment or accommodation in your research question and access to your cases but Eisenhardt and Graebner's (2007) advice is axiomatic in case study research. Providing a robust rationale for the selection of cases is a key aspect of the research strategy. You will need to write a section in your dissertation or thesis where you will demonstrate an understanding and evaluation of the options in the case study literature.

For the case study researcher, there are a number of types of cases to consider in addition to the number and the actual case or cases chosen. The basis for the choice is, as Flyvbjerg (2006) states, an information-oriented approach. Table 3.3 displays types of case study.

Table 3.3   Information-oriented approach to case study sampling

1	Extreme/deviant case	Obtains information on unusual cases, providing insight into the particularly problematic or the especially good.
2	Maximum variation case	Obtains information about the significance of various circumstances for case process and outcome, such as three to four cases that are very different on one dimension, e.g. location.
3	Critical case	Where theory has specified a clear set of propositions which the case can then test to support, challenge or extend the theory. Clearly, the theory has to be very strongly developed for this type of investigation. To achieve information about that permits logical deductions of the type 'If this is (not) valid for this case, then it applies to all (no) cases'.
4	Representative case	Can capture circumstances and conditions in an everyday situation. Well suited to student investigation in their workplace. Researcher has to be clear throughout about what the case(s) represents.
5	Revelatory case	Offers the researcher the opportunity to investigate a phenomenon which has previously been inaccessible.
6	Longitudinal case	Where the same case is studied over a period of time and data are captured at specific intervals. Shows how conditions have changed over the period of time.

Adapted from Flyvbjerg (2006)

In this table, where six types are depicted, the researcher can then develop the research strategy by matching the choice of type of case to the research problem/ question. The following research insight is an example of an extreme case.

Research insight: the Dutch film industry

A study into organizational memory took the form of case study research into latent organizations in the Dutch film industry. The authors described latent organizations as groups of individuals who regularly collaborate in short-term projects in the industry. These organizations have come about owing to the highly flexible working practices in the industry where access to work is uncertain. The authors, Ebbers and Wijnberg (2009), argued that by studying an extreme case, it would strengthen their argument that the phenomenon of the study also played a role in more regular organizations.

How many cases?

If the rationale for choice of case study is the illumination and extension of your conceptual framework, then the number of cases that you need can, to some extent, be answered at the same time. Nonetheless, how many cases remains a common question for students to ask their supervisors. A detailed argument for deciding how many cases to select for your research can be found in Yin (2009). He proposes that there are four types of case study design, based around a matrix of holistic, embedded, single and multiple cases. Figure 3.3 illustrates a simplified version of Yin's complex model which provides a basis for developing

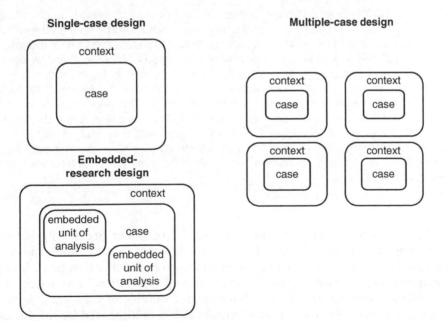

Figure 3.3   Case study designs

Adapted from Yin (2009)

a rationale for the case study research design. The researcher, according to this version, has three options for case study design. You will note that context appears in all the options, reminding us what case study research is all about. It may not be possible to fulfil the criteria for these cases completely, but these designs, nonetheless, provide guidance on how to prepare the rationale for the single case study design. First, there is choice of doing a single case study. Yin (2009) warns that in a single case study model, the case may not turn out to be quite the case that the researcher anticipated. He advises the researcher to prepare their arguments extremely thoroughly before embarking on a single case study design.

A second route is that of the embedded case study. An embedded case study involves more than one unit of analysis but usually within one organization. A large retail organization, for example, may be interested in finding out about how staff perceive the nature of customer service in their particular store. An embedded design would allow an in-depth investigation into this question across a number of units within a single organization, generating the subtle and rich data that characterizes case study research.

The third option presented in Figure 3.3 is the multiple case design, which enables the researcher to compare and contrast cases or explore the phenomenon in a number of different cases. We have already referred to one example of a multiple case (see research insight: click-and-mortar e-commerce). The following research insight provides another example of a multiple-case design.

Research insight: luxury wines

Beverland's (2005) study into brand authenticity sought to build theory through tracing the development of the brand history of luxury wine. His sampling criteria for the selection of his cases were derived from luxury brand characteristics drawn from the literature and included high price, excellent quality, specialized distribution channels and a prestige image. Following these criteria, the number of cases for his investigation was 26, which is an exceptionally high number in case study research. However, he clearly articulates the argument for this high number according to the above criteria and the study's epistemological approach. He collected data from interviews with respondents at their place of business, observations at the wineries and secondary data from the wine press, news media and the companies themselves. Further primary data were generated from 11 focus groups with luxury wine consumers and eight interviews with wine distributors.

In spite of this somewhat extreme example, more is not necessarily better in determining the number of cases. Beverland's data sets must be huge and take a great deal of managing, even from the experienced researcher that he is. It might be tempting to go down the positivist route and argue that more cases somehow address questions about the reliability and validity of the data. There are case study authors who argue that external validity is improved by several cases (for example, Leonard-Barton 1990; Voss et al. 2002). Interestingly, although Beverland's study consists of a very high number of cases, he does not argue for

Table 3.4 Choice and number of cases

Choice	Advantage	Disadvantage
Single case	Depth, insight, revelatory, unique	Evolving boundaries of case, arguments for the credibility and contribution of findings
Multiple case	Stronger arguments for 'validity' of study, evidence often considered more compelling Theory better grounded, more accurate	Less depth, possible need for additional resource, robust rationale need for choice of cases e.g. compare or contrast
Longitudinal case(s)	Ideal for tracking changing conditions	Resource heavy, requires significant commitment

Compiled from Eisenhardt and Graebner (2007) and Voss et al. (2002)

the contribution or quality of his work on the size of his sample, instead providing exhaustive information on the data sets, the analysis and of course the overall quality of the paper.

The data in each case (if you are choosing more than one) need to meet quality criteria and address any concerns of the reader through triangulation or whatever method you choose to argue for the relevance of your findings. The above table (Table 3.4) presents the practical as opposed to the theoretical considerations about the number of cases in the research design. In this table, longitudinal case or cases are argued to be a distinct research design owing to the lengthy data collection period and the resources involved. Note again the appearance of being able to argue for the validity of case study research through multiple-case study design. If you turn this 'question' around, then you might be able think about whether you are going to choose to do a single or multiple-case study design.

How would you argue, for example, that you chose multiple case studies just to make your work more valid? That seems to miss the point of case study research. If you are still unsure, revisit Table 3.2.

Your ontological and epistemological perspectives may influence your choice and if you are an interpretive thinker, you may find that single case suits your research perspective as well as your research objectives which may encompass such terms as 'explore in depth' and 'understand'. The more positivist researcher may be interested in objectives that feature words such as compare, contrast or even predict when the enquiry is to estimate the size of an effect (Woodside and Wilson 2003). If you do decide to do a single case study, make absolutely sure that you can argue strong grounds for this decision.

Piloting

There is also the question of piloting in case study research. Whilst piloting, which is the practice of trialling your research instruments prior to gathering your data, is widely recommended in research, the contextual dimension to case study research raises the question of whether piloting is appropriate. Baird (2004) describes how she conducted eight mini or pilot cases which involved field visits and interviews. Yin (2009) also discusses piloting although drawing a distinction between piloting and pretesting (usually a research instrument), where the pilot is a formative exercise assisting in the conceptual development of the enquiry. As many students are inexperienced in research, there is a strong argument for a trial. Weighed against this undoubtedly good practice is the need to finish within a specific and often alarmingly short timescale. The choice of a pilot case therefore needs to be based on criteria of convenience, easy access and proximity (Remenyi et al. 1998).

Triangulation

Triangulation, as mentioned in Chapter 1, is a critical part of many case study designs. It is a term derived from navigation and surveying where an area is divided into triangles, one side (the base line) and all angles of which are measured and the lengths of the other lines calculated trigonometrically (http://dictionary.reference.com). The following extract provides further description:

> Triangulation is based on finding an unknown location using angle measurements to two known locations. Mathematically, the two known positions define the two vertices (and length of the one side) of a triangle and the two bearing measurements define two of the angles of the triangle. These three things fix the size and orientation of the triangle; thus putting the unknown position at the third vertex of the triangle.
>
> (www.ion.org/satdiv/education/lesson6.pdf)

The principle in case study research is getting a fix on the phenomenon or, as it is referred to in the extract above, 'the unknown position' from two or more other points. This fix can be achieved through using the different methods and informants or even theory triangulation (Denzin 1978). The assumption underlying triangulation is multiple and independent measures (or other data) provide a more 'certain portrayal' of the phenomenon that is being studied (Jick 1979). However, there is more than one type of triangulation and Table 3.5 captures four main types of triangulation.

The first type of data triangulation consists of gathering data from different sources, for example interviewing managers and staff over a period of time in an investigation into organizational response to change. The same method of interviewing is used but with different sources of data. The second type of triangulation involves more than one researcher. An example of this type of triangulation might be a large funded

Table 3.5　Types of triangulation

Type	Description
Data	Data gathering from different sources, possibly at different times on the same object
Investigator	Use of more than one researcher in gathering and interpretation of data with same objective
Theoretical	Use of more than one theoretical perspective in the interpretation of a single data set
Method	Within-method (multiple techniques with same method) or between-method (different methods) with same object

Compiled from Denzin (1978), Jick (1979) and Wang and Duffy (2009)

research project where a team of researchers were involved in a multiple-case investigation into accounting systems. In theoretical triangulation, greater insight may be gained from looking at a data set from a number of theoretical perspectives. The final type of triangulation is methodological which, as the table indicates, is either within-method or between-method. Within-method triangulation consists of multiple techniques within a given method, for example several focus groups. Between-method triangulation uses different methods which might consist of a survey of an appropriate sample and analysis of documents. It is this version of triangulation which is particularly common in case study research. The following research insight provides an example of methodological triangulation.

Research insight: triangulating methods

A study into relational benefits in a football club adopted a single-case study approach (an extreme case) where a small club had been able to win various awards for family engagement. The data were generated from two main sources. First, there were interviews with the families who participated in a range of club activities. Secondary data about the club were accessed from the Football Association website and publications, consultancy reports and the club's own information about attendance and participation. The researchers were able from the two data sources to illustrate and extend theory into the third point in the triangle: family relational benefits in football.

Findings from different data sources saying the same thing provides the researcher with a basis for arguing that the research is credible. As Jick (1979: 603) argues, 'triangulation can capture a more complete, holistic and contextual portrayal of the units under study'. The data sources that are intended to support your research need to be mapped early in the research planning. For example, how will findings from a survey complement data generated through focus groups (between-methods triangulation)? What outline procedures have you in place for analysing these quite different data sources? What is the enveloping methodological approach that will allow you to argue for the consistency of your research? This final one is critical, as it provides the firm foundation for the whole of your enquiry which, like the spine discussed earlier, holds the study together.

Rather typically with research methods and underpinning philosophies, there is some controversy. Yin, in showing how evidence converges, states that it contributes to establishing 'facts' (2009: 118) but facts are something of an anathema to an interpretivist researcher, becoming all too close to a view that there is some objective reality. This notion is reiterated by Lee and Lings (2008) who argue that the principle of triangulation which is drawn from natural sciences and hence a positivist stance assumes that there is an external reality on which you can get the fix on your phenomenon. Where does this leave the researcher, especially the interpretivist one? It does not necessarily mean that you cannot argue for the credibility of your research using triangulation but it does signify that you have to be aware of the underlying philosophical arguments in research and provide an account of why triangulation has allowed your largely interpretivist study to be credible. This point will be returned to in Chapter 6.

Research quality

This is a topic which again runs through the whole book. It is not something that can be done retrospectively. Quality and how you as a researcher are going to demonstrate it needs to be understood and addressed from the very beginning. Quality is discerned by the reader both in the little things, such as presentation and spelling, as well as solid research design. However, no amount of proofreading can overcome weaknesses in research design and execution. You will need to have a plan of how your research strategy will 'hit' the quality notes which can range from the strength of your conceptual framework to the detail of your data analysis. Once more, there is no short cut and I would tell if you if there was anything that could circumvent the process. You will see in reading academic publications the lengths that the writers have gone to to convince the reader that their research meets the most stringent tests.

Case study research strategies are very varied in their execution, as you will note in your reading. In this chapter, we have explored the building blocks that you need to use in creating your research strategy. By having a strategy in place at an early stage in your research, you will be in a better position to cope with the inevitable problems that arise during the course of your research. Throughout your dissertation or thesis, you will argue for the quality and credibility of your research, referring to examples of good practice in your referencing and following accepted protocols. From the very beginning, you need to reassure your readers/examiners that you have embedded in your research design key quality markers that they will recognize.

Summary

- The formulation of a research question and objectives derived from the literature is essential for case study research.
- The development of a conceptual framework from the literature explains the focus of the research and guides the creation of the research strategy.
- The number of cases that you select in your study will largely depend on your research objectives/conceptual framework and have to be closely argued.
- Triangulation can provide arguments for the credibility of your research but you have to be aware of the philosophical assumptions of research traditions.

Exercises

1 Write down your research question, checking that it includes a 'how' or a 'why'. Draft three to four research propositions that stem from your research question based on your reading so far.
2 Locate an example of a study that has adopted a case study strategy. Check the research question/aim/objectives to see what words they contain that suggest a case study strategy. What type of case is it and how does its selection allow for the extension of the concepts that it studies?
3 Locate two academic papers that exemplify a single-case study design and a multiple-case study design. Note down the research question and objectives and how the method has developed from the objectives. What limitations do the authors state for the research? How might they have been overcome?

Key words

A conceptual framework underpins your research and is a construction that you build from the literature that relates very closely to your research objectives.

Triangulation refers to the process of bringing together the methods or data sets in your case study research that you can use to support your arguments for the quality of it.

Further reading

Leonard-Barton, D. (1990) 'A dual methodology for case studies: synergistic use of longitudinal single site with replicated multiple sites', *Organizational Change*, 1, 3, 248–266.
Oliver, P. (2008) *Writing Your Thesis*, second edition, London: Sage Publications.
Yin, R. (2009) *Case Study Research: Design and Methods*, fourth edition, Thousand Oaks, CA: Sage Publications.

References

Adelaar, T., Bouwman, H. and Steinfield, C. (2004) 'Enhancing customer value through click-and-mortar e-commerce: implications for geographical market reach and customer type', *Telematics and Informatics*, 21, 167–182.
Baird, M. (2004) 'Comparing cases: studies of commitment systems in Australia and the United States', *International Journal of Human Resource Management*, 15, 3, 433–444.
Beverland, M. (2005) 'Crafting brand authenticity: the case of luxury wines', *Journal of Management Studies*, 42, 5, 1003–1029.
Denzin, N. (1978) *The Research Act in Sociology*, second edition, Chicago, IL: Aldine.
Ebbers, J. and Wijnberg, N. (2009) 'Organizational memory: from expectations memory to procedural memory', *British Journal of Management*, 20, 478–490.
Eisenhardt, K. (1989) 'Building theories from case study research', *Academy of Management Review*, 14, 4, 532–550.
Eisenhardt, K. and Graebner, M. (2007) 'Theory building from cases: opportunities and challenges', *Academy of Management Journal*, 50, 1, 25–32.
Flyvbjerg, B. (2006) 'Five misunderstandings about case study research', *Qualitative Inquiry*, 12, 2, 219–245.
Halinen, A. and Törnroos, J-A. (2005) 'Using case methods in the study of contemporary business networks', *Journal of Business Research*, 58, 1285–1297.
Jick, T. (1979) 'Mixing qualitative and quantitative methods: triangulation in action', *Administrative Science Quarterly*, 24, 4, 602–611.
Lähdesmäki, M. and Siltaoja, M. (2010) 'Towards a variety of meanings: multiple representations of reputation in the small business context', *British Journal of Management*, 21, 207–222.
Lee, N. and Lings, I. (2008) *Doing Business Research: A Guide to Theory and Practice*, London: Sage Publications.
Leonard-Barton, D. (1990) 'A dual methodology for case studies: synergistic use of longitudinal single site with replicated multiple sites', *Organizational Change*, 1, 3, 248–266.
Maylor, H. and Blackmon, K. (2005) *Researching Business and Management*, Basingstoke: Palgrave Macmillan.
Myers, M. (2009) *Qualitative Research in Business and Management*, Thousand Oaks, CA: Sage Publications.
Olkkonen, R. (2001) 'Case study: the network approach to international sports sponsorship arrangement', *Journal of Business and Industrial Marketing*, 16, 4, 309–329.

Remenyi, D., Williams, B., Money, A. and Swartz, E. (1998) *Doing Research in Business and Management: An Introduction to Process and Method*, London: Sage Publications.

Stake, R. (1995) *The Art of Case Study Research*, Thousand Oaks, CA: Sage Publications.

Voss, C., Tsikriktsis, N. and Frohlich, M. (2002) 'Case research in operations management', *International Journal of Operations and Production Management*, 22, 2, 195–219.

Wang, W. and Duffy, A. (2009) 'A triangulation approach for design approach', *International Conference on Engineering Design*, Stanford, CA.

Woodside, A. and Wilson, E. (2003) 'Case study research methods for theory building', *Journal of Business and Industrial Marketing*, 18, 6/7, 493–508.

Yin, R. (2009) *Case Study Research: Design and Methods*, fourth edition, Thousand Oaks, CA: Sage Publications.

Access and Ethics in Case Study Research

4

Learning outcomes

At the end of this chapter, the reader will be able to:

- plan how to negotiate access to cases for research;
- prepare materials for obtaining ethical approval for research;
- understand the requirements of acting ethically and professionally with case study organizations;
- provide an account of the ethical processes conducted during the course of the research.

Introduction

The aim of this chapter is to cover the key areas of negotiating access for your research and of ensuring that your research process follows guidelines set down by universities, research councils and professional bodies. These two activities are closely linked. For organizations to grant you access to the data that you need for a credible piece of research, they need to be reassured that you will act responsibly. If you demonstrate a sound knowledge of ethical procedures and have supporting documentation then access, although not guaranteed, becomes less challenging. For case study research into business phenomena, students and researchers will often need to be connected closely to organizations to understand the complexity and context of the research that they are conducting. They will be spending time at the organization and need access to a range of data sources. Negotiating access to these organizations is therefore indispensable.

The first part of this chapter details ways in which you might negotiate access to organizations for your case study research. The second section deals with ethical research.

Negotiating access

Negotiating access is time-consuming and emotionally challenging and will require a great deal of preparation. Whether access to an organization or organizations is achieved through existing contacts or through 'cold calling', you are advised to follow the systematic procedures that are discussed in this chapter.

Your research strategy will already contain information about your data sources but now is the time to 'firm' this up. The organizations that you will be contacting will need to have as much detail as possible about what you require from them, how you plan to work and your timescales. We discussed the selection of cases in the previous chapter and so we will not return to it again in this chapter on the assumption that you have thought this through carefully by now. If you have not, please return to the preceding chapter. The process of negotiating access is one of the many occasions where research involves doing several things simultaneously. The research process is not linear in spite of the way that it is presented (we have to present it somehow!) and in order for it all to hang together, sometimes you have to be engaged with a number of things at the same time.

Preparation

The more that you think ahead and plan, the greater the likelihood of gaining and maintaining access to your chosen organizations. Essentially, what you are trying to establish is trust and your planning has to convey to organizations that you are approaching that you are a trustworthy individual and that you are representing a trustworthy organization (usually your university or place of study). Although it is always tempting to leap into action and try to set up appointments and interviews, an investment in thinking things through, reading, making notes and consultations with supervisors will reap dividends. With preparation in mind, it is worth noting that access may be something of a misnomer for this aspect of research as it does not convey the lengthy and complex process of a case study. A better word may be 'participation' or even 'partnership' as both these words imply a longer-lasting relationship, which is probably going to generate the kind of data that case study research is designed to elicit. An organization is more likely to support your research over a period of time, if you can supply it with detailed information about its role, the data you need and how much time the research on site is going to take. Researchers need to understand the organizational perspective on granting access. Any organization that grants you access will incur costs, for example allowing time for interviews and/or providing documents and information. These organizations quite understandably will be looking one way or another at how they may recover or, at least, justify these costs or looking at other benefits of participating in your research. Adapting some guidelines from Easterby-Smith et al. (2008), it is helpful at this stage if:

- The project has potential relevance and benefits the organization.
- The time and resources requested are minimal.
- The project appears not to be politically sensitive from an organizational perspective.
- The individuals concerned and/or the institutions have a good reputation.

These points all need to be crafted into the documentation that you will present to the organizations that you hope to persuade to participate. It is possible that the organization may have a mission to assist in research or education, so it is worth looking to see if any of the organizations that you have included in your sample have signed up for this type of activity. Equally, organizations who are experiencing tough times financially, attracting criticism or are in the throes of take-over or acquisition are not likely to be in a position of supporting research and so are best avoided.

If your research is concerned with a company in these situations, then you may have created a problem for yourself and you may wish to rethink. If you are planning to research cases that involve famous names/brands, note that these companies are inundated with requests asking them to assist in student research, so think very carefully about your research if you are dependent on working with an organization that is termed 'hard' access. Organizations are also aware that research often involves some form of critical evaluation and so would rather just not run the risk of any of the criticism 'leaking' into the wider world (Davies 2007). Conforming to the ethical protocols that are set out in the next section, especially those concerned with confidentiality, may address some of these reservations on the part of potential research cases or organizations. A researcher can ill afford for an organization to pull out of the research, although even with the best laid plans this may still happen. If you prepare and anticipate well, then the chances of this outcome are reduced. The following research insight provides an illustration of preparing to access organizations.

Research insight: supporting the community

Marina was studying how management accountants approached the implementation of new accounting practices in five medium-sized enterprises for her M.Res degree. For this multiple-case study, she needed to approach at least a dozen different companies in both the public and private sectors. Unsurprisingly, she was anxious about her ability to arrange access to this number of companies. She drew up a short but comprehensive review of the length of research project, the sources of data (number and length of management interviews, secondary data sources) and the number and duration of visits. As part of a 'thank you' to the organizations, she planned to offer a seminar at the end of her research to the senior managers in the participating organizations. She studied the websites of the organizations and drew up a script for the initial phone calls to discover the identity of the gatekeepers. When she had identified these people, she wrote formal letters to them personally with all the documentation that she had had approved by the university ethics committee. She was pleasantly surprised when two of the companies she applied to readily granted her access.

Given the assistance that participating organizations are going to afford you, it seems reasonable to think about a means of alleviating the costs they will incur during your research project. This can be done in two ways – first, by providing the participating organization with a very clear and detailed outline of your research and what you would need them to do and/or provide. Table 4.1 overleaf contains suggestions for an access pack and the materials that you might think to include in it.

I have suggested that you include your *curriculum vitae* (CV) as the organizations will need to know about you, the researcher, so tell them about your professional and research experience. If you put together an access pack, it demonstrates to potential partnership organizations that you have thought things through and that you are a well prepared and organized person. You can include the access pack in your dissertation or thesis appendix where it will convey the same message to the reader/examiner. Second, you should offer some means of recompense, such as an overview of your research findings in a written report or in a seminar or both. If you are a student, you should be acting as a professional, dressing and communicating appropriately. Nonetheless, be prepared for a demanding time and even if you do manage to negotiate

Table 4.1   Example of an access pack (electronic and paper)

Research question, objectives and practical outcomes
Covering letter to the gatekeeper giving an overview of the research
Number and types of cases: so that they can see what other types of organizations might be participating
Detailed information about the direct and indirect data needed for the case: interviews, documents, meetings, observation, survey
Informants: managers of which departments, staff
Anticipated time on site: number of visits and duration
Facilities: desk, e-mail
Letters of informed consent (university letter-headed paper)
Researcher CV and contact details of supervisor
Outline of slides for a seminar

access, you may encounter staff within the organization who are less than helpful. This lack of co-operation may arise from a political situation within the organization and other than being flexible and smiling a lot, there is not a great deal that you can do about it.

Reaching out

In planning access, researchers are strongly advised to use existing contacts for their research or, as Maylor and Blackmon (2005: 270) describe them, 'warm contacts'. Returning to the model of stakeholders and relationships in Chapter 1 (Figure 1.1), stakeholder groups in your research are your family, your friends and your employers or former employers. Think about the connections that these groups have with organizations and whether these connections might be able to provide you with suitable cases. Build up this list, sorting out the relative 'warmth' of these connections, what the connection consists of and the suitability of the organizations that your connections represent. You will understand why people spend so much time 'networking'. You will then be able to work your way through the list, ticking off ones to follow up and ones to cross off. If these connections do not yield any results for your case selection or sample, you will have to negotiate access the hard way or 'cold'. At this stage, before access or the partnerships have been agreed, it is advisable to have flexibility in your proposal as illustrated in the following research insight.

Research insight: mobile technology

Rafael wanted to study how sales teams in the field were using mobile technology. He argued in his proposal that three case companies would allow him to compare how the technology was being deployed. He had access to one company through a member of his tennis club, who was a senior manager in a building supplies company and which had recently invested in mobile technology for its sales teams. So one company was able to provide material for one of the cases but what about the remaining two? Rafael

(Continued)

(Continued)

was able to obtain the details of a contact from his tennis colleague and so got in touch with the second company. This company was concerned about a single researcher working in a rival company having access to what might be sensitive data, so Rafael was not successful there. Rafael stopped to think at this point and realized he had to address this question of confidentiality of data. He then re-wrote his research outline which made explicit reference to how confidentiality would be maintained and prepared an access pack of his research. He then approached a third company, on this occasion 'cold'. Upon reading the research outline, the company questioned Rafael further about confidentiality and being satisfied with the responses was prepared to provide him with the access that he needed. Rafael thought carefully about his research objectives and, after discussion with his supervisor, decided that he could still achieve his research objectives with two units or cases and so embarked on his research.

Stating matters rather brutally, you need the participating organization more than they need you and so you have to build a case or argument detailing why they should support you and your research. Make sure that the arguments for participation can be clearly articulated in an interview. Practice your persuasive powers with friends and colleagues. You will probably be negotiating with a senior manager who, if you are fortunate, will be in a position to grant you access. This person will need to continue to support you and your research, going on to open further doors for you. This person is your sponsor and it is good practice to get back to your sponsor with broad anonymized results or findings to reassure them that their decision has been vindicated. It is worth trying to find out what the sponsor's motivations are for sponsoring your research. If the sponsor has an agenda which is not consistent with you achieving your research aims, then there is really little point in continuing, however unfortunate this is. This is unacceptable and unethical behaviour but there is little that you can do about it other than discuss it with your supervisor and learn from it (Maylor and Blackmon 2005)!

Collecting the evidence

In planning your research, you will have to have thought ahead about how you are going to collect and analyse the data (see Chapters 5 and 6) and, as Remenyi et al. (1998) suggest, how you are going to triangulate your data. You can think which data you need to collect directly, such as focus group data and data that can be collected indirectly such as survey data or accessing secondary data. The costs of direct data collection are going to be higher for the participating organization(s) so, in planning your data collection, think about how these costs can be minimized or shown to be central to your project. Case study research is characterized by mixed methods, since the researcher can be sensitive to the concerns of the participating organizations in a number of data sources. When you are compiling your access pack, balance the need for access to information with an acknowledgement of the organization's perspective (see Table 4.1). Be prepared to be flexible but not to the extent of compromising your research objectives. Your evidence will be collected at various levels within the organization and the following research insight is an e-mail from a student to her supervisor reporting on her access progress in her case study.

Research insight: Linda's blog

Hi

I have met up with three banks so far who have given me a lot of information and continue to send me electronic documents. I may end up talking to five banks, as two more banks have taken interest in my research and would like to meet up. X bank pulled out, my contact changed jobs and no one seems to know how to take it forward. I have also been introduced to some of those I'll be interviewing. It's actually gone more smoothly than I anticipated so that's been a relief. I was hoping to set up a blog so you can see my daily activities, but haven't been able to get round to it. I have set up an appointment for one informal interview with the Corporate Communications Manager of Y Bank for tomorrow, and am currently drafting my questions. If it's OK with you, I'll e-mail it to you by the end of the day, so you can feed back?

Linda

You will note in the e-mail how, even at this early stage of the research, the situation has changed. Your contacts will change jobs but, at the same time, news of your research may spread through informal channels and new opportunities emerge. Also note the intention in this research insight to set up a blog which would be very useful in recording progress and in due course add substance to your research.

Although you may have obtained consent from management to conduct your research, you still have to obtain your data from survey respondents, interview data from informants and documents from whoever is responsible for keeping them. It is important to remember that you are an outsider, even if you work for the organization as, for your research, you are adopting a different role which may influence how people perceive you. If you want to collect data that are useful, i.e. address your research question, be discrete and considerate. Be alert to some people testing your probity (Bryman 2001) and make sure that things that you are told are not innocently repeated. Also be aware of mission creep or, more accurately, research creep where the organization or staff within it ask you to extend or adapt your research so it fits some agenda of their own rather than yours. If this happens, discuss it with your sponsor, even if it is them who are asking you to do it along with your supervisor.

You cannot expect your supervisors to be able to arrange access for you. Their role in your research has been discussed in Chapter 1. They may have some contacts for access but you cannot expect it. No matter how carefully you have done your access preparations, some companies will just not allow you access for reasons which are nothing to do with you. You just have to be prepared for this. All this preparation and planning may seem very time-consuming when you are keen to get started with your research but this preliminary work cannot be skipped. The preparation is a matter of improving your chances rather than creating certainties. As a researcher, the author has never been able to gain access to a few financial services companies whilst others have been more than helpful over a period of years. This partnership has been based on trusting relationships developed where they have repeatedly demonstrated the ethical nature of their research.

Ethical research

All participants in the research process should feel that the research has, at the very least, caused no harm. It may be better still to have a feeling that it has in some way made a contribution to the participating organizations. This contribution could be a tangible outcome that the participating organization(s) can appreciate such as a report or seminar. It can consist of a feeling of well-being in the organizations that they have participated in a worthwhile activity. It is your role to convince them of this. Your time 'in the field' will give you some sense of how you can make this contribution. Ethical research in business forms part of the research process. Research students are expected to submit a research ethics form to the university research ethics committee for approval. It is also expected that you write a section in your research methods chapter. This section will detail the steps that you took to make sure that your research adhered to ethical guidelines.

Confidentiality forms one of the cornerstones of conducting research which conforms to ethical principles. As a researcher, you may learn from your informants or from documents about personal opinions and private thoughts as well as competitive intelligence. Informants often like to talk about their jobs and working life. Your data may therefore contain material which, if thoughtlessly handled, could cause your informants, your participating case or even yourself harm. All researchers need to think carefully about the people who are involved in research and whether there are any activities which should or should not be engaged in (Bryman 2001). Again, stopping to think about who you are talking to, what data you are collecting, how you are capturing and storing the data all form the foundations of ethical research. You must store all data and the back-up copies of the data securely. There have been many stories reported of the loss of storage devices and laptops with confidential data. Do not let this happen to you. The principle of not causing harm is central to ethical research with further arguments that research should be beneficial to participants. How can you, as a case study researcher, avoid causing harm and create benefits?

Deception and covert research

Investigations that involve any form of deception or disguise are indicators that ethical protocols may be being violated. In marketing, for example, the 'mystery shopper' is a common method of assessing service levels in organizations, where a researcher poses as a shopper or customer, usually for a client organization, to ascertain usual levels of service. The whole premise is founded on the notion that the staff, who deliver the service, do not know that their performance is being assessed. The professional association that governs the profession has stated that:

> The Mystery Shopper Professional Association (MSPA) expects members and shoppers to follow principles of honesty, professionalism, fairness and confidentiality to guard the interests of the public and our clients in order to promote good business practices. (mspa-eu.org/en/ethics.html)

Although there are documented examples of research that involved deception (for example, Goode 1996), deception in case study research where relationships and intimacy become established could be highly problematic. This is particularly true for the researcher who is studying their own organization, where any degree of deception or covertness would impact on their working life. If some degree of deception is absolutely unavoidable, then one way to address it is to thoroughly debrief anyone involved or affected by the research afterwards (Saunders et al. 2007). A rather obvious means of data collection in case study research is observation. Observation in research takes two broad forms – participant and non-participant. Participant observation is probably more likely in a case study where you are 'working' with the people that you are observing. Non-participant observation occurs when the researcher is outside the research setting. You have to be open about the overall purpose of the data collection that is being conducted but you can prove to be non-specific about any detail. The more quickly you anonymize the data the better, that is separating out the names of any staff and the data. Coding in advance further reduces any risk of data and people being connected (see Chapter 6).

Research councils fund prestigious research projects in the UK and provide the following guidelines for the researchers, who receive their funding.

Research insight: ethical research

1 Research should be designed, reviewed and undertaken to ensure integrity, quality and transparency.
2 Research staff and participants must normally be informed fully about the purpose, methods and intended possible uses of the research, what their participation in the research entails and what risks, if any, are involved.
3 The confidentiality of information supplied by research participants and the anonymity of respondents must be respected.
4 Research participants must take part voluntarily, free from any coercion.
5 Harm to research participants must be avoided in all instances.
6 The independence of research must be clear, and any conflicts of interest or partiality must be explicit.

(See, for example, www.esrc.ac.uk/_images/Framework_for_Research_Ethics_tcm8-4586.pdf)

The guidelines provide a template for all researchers in all types of research whether case study or not and, in the following section, each principle is discussed.

Integrity, quality and transparency

Your research intentions must be honestly stated to participants and to everybody concerned, for example supervisors and doctoral committees. Covert research, that is, when the research may not be entirely openly conducted, is discussed below. Even if the findings of your research are not quite what you anticipated, they must be reported accurately. If the research has been conducted in accordance with the accepted research conventions, then your findings will be of interest and relevance. All your actions need to be clear to participants and accounted for in your final research submission. Doctoral examiners and journal editors need to be satisfied about research instruments, for example questionnaires, samples or selections of respondents, data analysis, particularly with qualitative research, and the conclusions that are drawn from these data. Reviewers expect to see this type of detail in submissions. The quality of your research will be based on the research methods that you follow, the sources that you consult and scrupulous citing of all these sources.

Informed participation (consent)

For case study research, there are two levels of informed consent. First, informed consent forms part of the negotiation process, usually with a gatekeeper, who may seek reassurance about organizational concerns. The second level of informed consent will apply to those who provide the data, whether primary or secondary. All your participants need to be made fully aware of their role in the research, how the data that they provide will be presented or used and that they can withdraw from the research at any time. Researchers could provide an interview guide if that forms part of the data collection. All research staff engaged in the research must assess their own situation in terms of safety and potential risk, both physical and psychological. No one should find themselves in situations where they are uncomfortable, intimidated or threatened in any way or where provision of data is in some way conditional upon researcher co-operation. Careful planning of research should include awareness of the 'safety' of the researcher, that is physical and emotional. If you do encounter a situation in which you are uncomfortable, discuss it as a matter or urgency with your supervisor. No research is so important that you should continue in a position where you are uncomfortable. Researchers also need to be aware of diversity in the research participants, covering such areas as ethnicity, gender, class and culture (Davies 2007). Sensitivity and an awareness of the views and perspectives of your research participants may help to address some of the hurdles that the researcher usually has to overcome.

Confidentiality and anonymity

Superficially, ensuring confidentiality and maintaining anonymity seem to be quite straightforward but the researcher needs to be aware of pitfalls. Confidential means secret. So how does the researcher ensure this when the publication or dissemination of their research is an essential element of the research process? The following suggestions can help the researcher balance the demands of confidentiality and the publishing of the research:

- The name and details of participants should only be revealed with the consent of the participant.
- Participants are referred to by a pseudonym (including the name of the organization or location).
- Data and details of informants should either be separated from the data and/or kept secure.
- E-mails including attachments, are not secure and care should be taken in the writing and storing of research e-mails.

The following insight describes an investigation in the financial services sector.

Research insight: confidential and some

Marylou researched management development in financial services organizations using case studies as her research strategy. She needed to give details about the participating organizations (four) such as core activities (insurance, retail banking), approximate turnover, management structure and geographical spread as possible influences on management development policies. Although the participating organizations were given pseudonyms in her dissertation, she had to be very careful about the amount of information that she provided in her research about these organizations as informed readers might be able to work out who the participating organizations actually were.

Ensuring anonymity of participants and organizations extends beyond providing pseudonyms to concealing any detail that might betray the participants' real identity. A further consideration for the researcher is to remember that all the information gleaned in a study or project is *privileged*, i.e. the researcher has been awarded special rights to carry out the research. The organizations with whom you are working may require you to sign a confidentiality agreement. Read it carefully and check that you can still publish work from the data that you collect. You are advised to ensure that you have explicit agreement at the outset with regard to publishing your work that covers anonymity, the right to read and comment on publications and any right to veto (Easterby-Smith et al. 2008).

Research participants

Research participants should consent to the research by being informed formally and in advance, which is best accomplished through the practice of informed consent. They can then have time to think through their decision and it allows them to feel in control. If potential participants decide not to join in the research project or decide for any reason to pull out, they should not feel in any way disadvantaged or guilty. The researcher should make an appropriate acknowledgement of their consideration or participation to that point. What constitutes participation in research? In most cases, participants will probably supply primary data through interviews, focus groups or surveys. However, there may also be instances of where participants facilitate research through providing access to people, documents, electronic sources and meetings. As we have discussed in earlier chapters, secondary data are particularly valuable in business research and case study research in particular. Ethical principles, of course, extend into the realm of secondary data collection just as much as primary. Minutes of meetings may yield helpful data for the researcher but all the rules that are discussed in this chapter apply to reporting or including meeting data, such as anonymity, consent, confidentiality and transparency.

Students, usually those studying part-time or following blended learning models, often choose to conduct research in their own organization. There may be a number of reasons for this decision that can range from convenience to a desire to explore a particular problem or question. There are unique ethical issues that arise from doing a case study in your own organization. Creswell (2007) expresses concerns about power and risk in this situation and this would be particularly relevant where the students are MBA or DBA and where they will probably be managers in organizations. The implications of managers researching within their own organizations are that potential participants who are less senior may perceive that power is unevenly balanced in the researcher's favour. They may feel that they have to take part in the research and that they have to say certain things. Risk can occur to the researcher where their position may be permanently eroded, to the informants, those who do not participate and, finally, to the quality of the data which may be biased at collection and at analysis. The researcher working for the organization has to make a careful trade-off between the benefits of access and those of ethics and independence. As a researcher pursuing ethical research guidelines, you have to balance access or convenience with these risks as well as the quality of the data and hence research.

Do some good

From time to time, researchers may find themselves working with participants in research who could be considered vulnerable. The concept and perception of power plays a role in much research but particularly with vulnerable participants where they may feel that they cannot withhold consent or withdraw even though they feel uncomfortable. Children participating in research may not fully appreciate what participation in research may involve. Research where children form a source of data is best left to professional and/or experienced researchers. With vulnerable participants, it is particularly important that the research benefits them in some way.

Research insight: fancy footwork

Laura was interested in how a certain football club managed to have a regular home crowd that exceeded that of its rivals in the league. Her initial enquiries suggested that this was an exemplary case. The club ran after-school and holiday clubs for the children in the area and it appeared that these activities contributed to the first-team match-day attendance. In order to understand the relationship between the two, she needed to interview children and families. Her research ethics proposal to the university had to include a specific statement about how the research would not only do no harm but in fact would benefit the young participants. The children were interviewed with their parents, eliciting their views first before moving on to their parents, so that their replies were not overly influenced by their parents. The children felt that their views were important in the research and their participation valued.

By studying this club and its innovative methods of engaging family participation, the researcher argued that the case provided theoretical contributions to relationship marketing and practitioner guidance to other football league clubs. In the research insight above, the researcher had been specially trained to interview children. Interviewing vulnerable participants may lead to difficulties with university ethics committees unless there are exceptional circumstances. If you have thoughts about involving anyone who could be deemed a vulnerable participant, this is something that needs to be discussed very early on in your research with your supervisor.

Independence of research

Case study researchers will find that they are working closely with the organizations that form the units of study. They spend a lot of time on site, building relationships with staff, gaining trust and sharing some of the problems, especially in longitudinal case studies. You will need to ensure that you are very discrete in any conversations that you might have informally about your research. This is particularly true if you are using observation as a means of collecting data. It is therefore all too easy to become too close to the case in a way that the non-case study generation researchers may not. At the same time, the benefit of case study research is, as you have learnt, to generate rich, insightful data. The researcher may even come under a little pressure from the organization to present the findings in a flattering light. No matter the style of research, whether interpretive or positivist, the independence of the researcher and their report/dissertation has to be maintained for their research to be credible and rigorous. Having established an 'ethical trail', that is, by acting in accordance with ethical guidelines throughout, the researcher should be in a strong position to argue for the integrity of the research.

Digital research

The digital world has transformed research in terms of accessing sources and in storing and manipulating files. This section suggests some areas of good practice for working in a digital environment.

Researching using the internet may present opportunities of ease of access, time-saving and overall convenience. You may, for example, decide to survey staff using an internet-based questionnaire, study an interchange of e-mails on a chosen topic or set up a website to manage the research project. Some specific questions arise from internet-based research that may impact on case study research, such as who or what exactly is the subject of the research, whether it is the author of the material or interactions (aoir.org/reports/ethics 2002).

As part of your data collection, you could decide to host or access a newsgroup within your participating organizations as a means of eliciting opinions and views about your research objectives. Behaving appropriately online in such fora is often referred to as netiquette and refers to the set of conventions that users of the forum abide by. Although netiquette is not the same thing as research ethics, it is concerned with respect and trust, therefore a brief discussion is included here. Hall et al. (2004) recognize six issues of importance where netiquette is concerned:

1 The use of subject header used in any posting to a newsgroup can reduce the risk of misunderstandings between the researcher and newsgroup members.
2 Self-identification and self-presentation of the researcher are critical, as readers will form their evaluations about the credibility of the research and the researcher based on this. A formal verifiable, disclosed identity of the researcher, for example through a link to an institutional website, can increase the credibility of the researcher's claimed identity and shows respect and courtesy to members of the newsgroup.
3 The researcher must be familiar with the common language used on the specific newsgroup, including jargon, abbreviations, acronyms, *emoticons* and common grammatical rules. The ability to speak the newsgroups' language shows respect to the rules and conventions of the group.

4 The researcher should always ask appropriate questions, not ones that could have been answered by a library or archive search. To do this, the researcher must acquaint themselves on the subject matter before asking for help.

5 The specific culture of the newsgroup should be understood through online acclimatization or reading FAQs and archives in order to understand the nuances of group interactions.

6 The researcher has an obligation to be open and honest about the purpose, nature, procedures and risks of the research.

Ethical issues in research are complex and ongoing. The more aware you become about researching ethically, the more you are aware of the pitfalls and that you also run some risks. Although there are abundant guidelines, the researcher will probably find that the smaller issues are the ones that they have to resolve (Easterby-Smith et al. 2008). This point is reinforced by a study, which concludes that the reflexivity which qualitative researchers usually bring to their research should be extended into addressing ethical issues (Guillemin and Gillam 2004). The authors argue that reflexivity is a sensitizing notion that enables ethical practice to occur in complex research situations.

Learning how to store your data in line with ethical practices can also transform the way that you work. You may need to access your information at any stage of your research to present or update your stakeholders. The following insight has been offered by a colleague who is able to work effectively anywhere.

Research insight: working anywhere

As researchers, we often find ourselves working in a range of locations – from our university offices, at home, at conferences, on trains and aeroplanes. We may have our work PC, a home office PC and a laptop. Keeping track of our files and version control can be a challenge. Often at conferences you will find academics with memory sticks in each pocket desperately trying to find the one with the latest version of their presentation, and then mid-flow apologize that this one appears to be 'not the right one'. There are some possible solutions to this problem.

Find *one* memory stick with large enough memory, usually 2 gigabytes (GB) or more. Separate your work into files and folders (thematic grouping is good not only for research, but for everyday life!). To protect your files, encrypt your memory stick but do choose a memorable password, otherwise your data will become inaccessible. Keeping your password on a piece of paper near the memory stick defeats the purpose of password protecting your files and also runs foul of ethical practice. If you find yourself losing things, this option may not be for you. Contact your IT support department instead, and talk to them about protecting your files.

Once you have identified the files and folders that you will need at your disposal while away from the office, you can do the following:

- Always work from your memory stick files and folders, so that you have the latest file versions.
- At the end of your working day or session, back up the data onto your work PC, or (if secure) your laptop and home PC (simply copy the folders from your memory stick and paste them into a select folder location). In this way, you always have a back-up, should your memory stick break down or disappear.

(Continued)

(Continued)

You also have the option of using online document storage tools. Simply put an appropriate search term in any search engine and a link to online storage should appear. This is a great option, in particular if you are working on a joint research project and you wish your colleagues to contribute to a single version of your document.

Online storage often has a revision history where you can open previous versions of your files. This has the great benefit of not confusing the different versions of your documents. You can also go back to a previous draft. You do not need to worry about back-ups or losing data because the online facility is managing it for you.

(Contributed by Dr Petia Petrova)

It would be a mistake to take the view that once ethical approval has been gained for your research that you can forget about ethics. As Figure 4.1 demonstrates, adhering to ethical principles continues and permeates every aspect of your research.

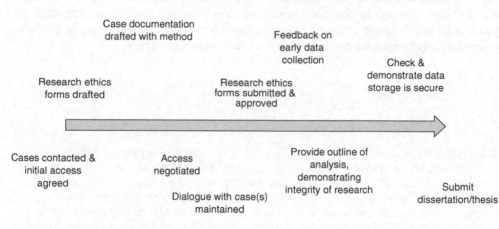

Figure 4.1   Continuity of research ethics

As always in attempting to depict processes in research, the process often appears linear when, probably, you will find that there is repetition and interruption in the process. For example, you may receive feedback on your research ethics application which could involve a re-draft. By following a model as shown in Figure 4.1, the honesty and integrity of your research is apparent throughout.

Summary

In this chapter, we have discussed how you might gain access to organizations where you are going to be able to collect the data that you need for your research. Preparation is everything and there is a great deal more work than you might think. You will need to allow plenty of time and devote a great deal of energy to this activity. Ethical research requires a great deal of planning as well as an understanding of how ethical principles need to be interpreted *in situ*.

- Gaining access to your case(s) is closely linked to ethical research as it involves issues of integrity, quality and transparency. Warm contacts should be explored first for access to cases.
- Time spent in careful preparation will improve chances of access and lessen the chances of participants withdrawing.
- Researching your own organization raises questions of power and risk that need to be thought addressed.
- The researcher's own security and safety must be considered.
- There is plenty of guidance about ethical research but small issues are likely to be the ones that are hardest to resolve.

Exercises

1 As part of preparing your research plan, provide three benefits of your research to a potential participating organization. How would you respond to the question that they might be harmful consequences?
2 Find example of letters of informed consent, identify examples of good practice and then draft your own letter to potential informants with specific reference to your planned data sources.
3 Draw up an outline of how your research is (a) doing no harm and (b) doing some good.

Key words

Access refers to the student being able to talk to informants, visit locations and any other data collection activities which they need in order to achieve their research objectives. In case study research, access to case(s) and the data sources that you need has to be formally arranged and maintained within the boundaries of ethical research.

Confidentiality in ethical research is a promise that the researcher makes to informants, participants and other stakeholders that you respect their participation and that you will ensure that all the information you have obtained remains secure and safe.

Anonymity is related to confidentiality and again is a promise that none of the information can be traced back to the supplier of that information.

Further reading

Goode, E. (1996) 'The ethics of deception in social research: a case study', *Qualitative Sociology*, 19, 11–33.

References

Bryman, A. (2001) *Social Research Methods*, New York: Oxford University Press.
Creswell, J. W. (2007) *Qualitative Enquiry and Research Design: Choosing Among Five Approaches*, Thousand Oaks, CA: Sage Publications.

Davies, M. (2007) *Doing a Successful Research Project*, Basingstoke: Palgrave Macmillan.

Easterby-Smith, M., Thorpe, R. and Jackson, P. (2008) *Management Research*, third edition, London: Sage Publications.

Goode, E. (1996) 'The ethics of deception in social research: a case study', *Qualitative Sociology*, 19, 11–33.

Guillemin, M. and Gillam, L. (2004) 'Ethics, reflexivity, and "Ethically Important Moments" in Research', *Qualitative Inquiry*, 10, 2, 261–280.

Hall, G. J., Frederick, D. and Johns, M. D. (2004) '"NEED HELP ASAP!!!": A feminist communitarian approach to online research ethics', in M. D. Johns, S. S. Chen and G. J. Hall (eds) *Online Social Research: Methods, Issues, and Ethics*, New York: Peter Lang. 239–253.

Maylor, H. and Blackmon, K. (2005) *Researching Business and Management*: Basingstoke: Palgrave Macmillan.

Remenyi, D., Williams, B., Money, A. and Swartz, E. (1998) *Doing Research in Business and Management: An Introduction to Process and Method*, London: Sage Publications.

Saunders, M., Lewis, P. and Thornhill, A. (2007) *Research Methods for Business Students*, fourth edition, Harlow: Pearson Education.

Data Collection

5

Learning outcomes

At the end of this chapter, the reader will be able to:

- evaluate the particular capabilities and deficiencies of individual data collection methods for case study research strategy;
- construct arguments for combining selected data collection methods, such as primary and secondary and qualitative and quantitative;
- provide a rationale for the data collection methods chosen for the case study research in achieving the research objectives;
- understand the role of triangulation in collecting and analysing data.

Introduction

The starting place for your data collection and analysis is to think about the quality and credibility of your research. Many students jump into data collection without sufficient thought about how the overall research process will be evaluated by readers and examiners. If you stop to think about how you will be arguing for the credibility of your data and findings before you collect your data, you will be dealing with some potentially catastrophic issues before they even arise. Case study research is characterized by multiple data sources, often consisting of different data collection techniques. In this chapter, the basic principles of data collection will be discussed within the specific context of case study research. This discussion is intended as an overview of techniques that are appropriate for case study research and how these techniques can work together to provide credible findings. Students are strenuously advised to read up in detail about individual methods, which are beyond the scope of this book. Suggestions of further reading are provided at the end of the chapter.

Methodology and methods

To maintain consistency in your research, the vocabulary of your research objectives and your data collection and analysis need to be in harmony. For example, if you are using words such as exploring or discovering, the choice of these words suggests to the reader/examiner that the research may contain an element of qualitative data. Similarly, if the objectives use such terminology as determine or test, then there is an expectation of quantitative data and measurement. Being very careful with your vocabulary and using research terms consistently conveys to your audience that you understand and can use appropriate research methods in addressing your research objectives.

The discussion in Chapter 2 on research philosophies provides an overview of the research paradigms. Your data collection methods should 'sit' more or less within one of these research paradigms, establishing an epistemological coherency. In Figure 5.1, Yin's (2009: 102) suggestions of data collection methods for case study research are grouped according to the research approach in which they are embedded. By embedding your data collection methods, you will then achieve a solid foundation to your research.

You will note that, in this figure, some data collection methods appear in more than one of the approaches. You will note that observation, for example, is common to all three approaches and this is because observation research can be adapted to fit the epistemology. It follows a positivist epistemology when the research objectives involve any form of measurement, so that the observation can consist of counting incidences of a chosen behaviour, such as the frequency of phone calls. Observation is a common method for interpretivists when they seek to immerse themselves in their study, making notes on behaviour, keeping a diary or recording conversations. For critical realist researchers, observation will form part of their approach, where their view of reality allows for some reconciliation between socially constructed meaning and an observable reality. As critical realism tends towards explanations that might try to demonstrate a causal relationship ('What caused the events associated with the phenomenon to occur?'), Easton (2010) argues that experimentation provides a possibility for recording actions of the recollections of those actions.

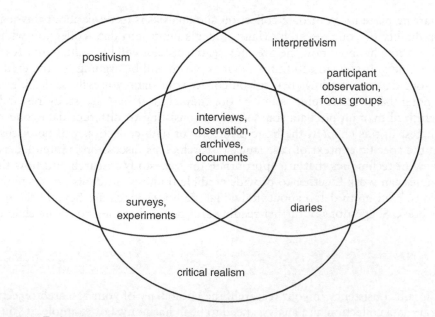

Figure 5.1   Embedding your methods in epistemological approaches

When developing your plan for data collection, you will have to bear in mind the number of cases in the study. You should aim to have similar methods of data collection across all your cases, so that you can make comparisons and/or observe differences based on similar data sources. Table 5.1 shows a simplified record of data collection across five SMEs. The study was concerned with how shortcomings in the IT fault repair service might contribute to high levels of staff turnover. The records capture the various stages of data collection in the ninth month of the study. This detail in data capture not only reminds the researcher exactly where they are in the research process but supports later claims for research quality (see Chapter 7).

The researcher has chosen four separate data sources as a means of addressing the research question: focus groups with IT users, an interview in each case with the IT manager, experiments with the systems and, finally, an analysis of IT reporting data in each of the organizations. Staff turnover data were analysed over a three-year period. You may prefer to record your data in another way but ensure that you make very accurate and detailed records. These records must be updated and amended throughout the period of study.

Your case study could therefore combine primary and secondary data sources, which consist of qualitative and quantitative data. Table 5.2 provides an overview of how the collection techniques in Figure 5.1 can subscribe to quantitative or qualitative data and how apparently similar techniques can be used to collect different types of data.

As Table 5.2 demonstrates, there is an extensive choice of methods for the case study researcher. Your research objectives will enable you to make some initial decisions about your methods. It is a valuable exercise to map your methods against your research objectives after discussion with your supervisors. Data sources and data collection will now be discussed in greater detail.

Table 5.1 Data collection in the ninth month of a five-case investigation

Data source	Case A	Case B	Case C	Case D	Case E
Focus groups with 8–10 IT users (qual.)	Month 5, two groups, data transcribed	Month 5, one group, second group organized	Month 6, two groups, data transcribed/ analysed	Month 7, one group, data transcribed	Month 7, two groups, recordings only
Interviews with IT manager or equivalent (qual.)	Month 9, one done	Month 10, five to go	Month 8, four done, one to go	Month 6, five completed and transcribed	Month 7, four completed
Experiment, five problems reported (quant.)	Month 11	Month 12	Month 12	Month 13	Month 13
IT fault data analysis (quant.) revenue and turnover data	Month 13	Month 13	Month 14	Month 14	Month 14

Table 5.2   Qualitative and quantitative data sources for case study research

Data	Qualitative data sources	Quantitative data sources
Primary	interviews (face to face, phone, online) focus groups, participant observation, diaries	survey, observation, experiment
Secondary	minutes of meetings, internal reports, consultancy reports, market research reports, government and EU data	spreadsheets, graphs, annual reports, external statistics, panel data, UK and EU data

Primary data

Primary data are new data which have been collected directly by the researcher(s) from original sources (Easterby-Smith et al. 2008; Remenyi et al. 1998) and specifically for the research project (Saunders et al. 2007). In collecting primary data, the researcher is aiming to generate new insights into the research question(s) with fresh data. Students also gain knowledge into the rigour of research methods which provides them with the lifelong skill of being able to interrogate data sources and evaluate research thoroughly. The strength of case study research is its capability of studying a research question or problem in depth and in context, therefore the data collection procedures should overall complement this characteristic. Although case study research is sometimes thought of as being a research strategy that consists of qualitative data, this strategy can actually employ various data collection procedures for within-case and cross-case comparison (Dooley 2002). As we have seen, case study research can be embedded in at least three research traditions (Figure 5.1), lending itself quite legitimately to quantitative and qualitative data collection. In this section, we shall be reviewing the various techniques that a case study researcher can use to collect primary data.

Figure 5.2 depicts three possible techniques for collecting primary data suitable for case study research: survey, observation and interview. Each technique is ostensibly 'neutral', therefore lending itself to quantitative or qualitative data collection, depending on how it fits with the overall research approach (see Figure 5.1). For each technique, you will need to develop an instrument, that is, the means by which you will collect your data. The research instrument also demonstrates that you have followed accepted protocols in your data collection and how you argue for the rigour of your data. Examples of a research instrument include a questionnaire, a guide for interviews or focus groups or an observation guide. Instruments designed to collect quantitative and qualitative data will usually differ in the degree of structure, for example a research instrument for a survey, usually referred to as a questionnaire, will be highly structured, requiring the respondent to answer closed questions (yes/no/I don't know). The qualitative version of a survey may have open questions where the respondent may use their own words in answering the questions.

To try and make life a little simpler, we shall discuss quantitative and qualitative data separately and, in the discussion, the various means of data collection have been assigned according to the most common way in which they are used.

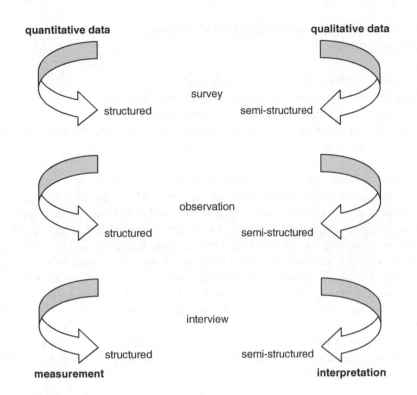

quantitative data   qualitative data

survey
structured   semi-structured

observation
structured   semi-structured

interview
structured   semi-structured

measurement   **interpretation**

Figure 5.2   Research instruments for primary data

Quantitative data

The key question underlying the collection and analysis of quantitative data is 'what are you measuring?' You will only have a clear idea of what you want to measure if you have prepared your theoretical groundwork through a thorough review of the literature. To measure, you will have to have identified the attributes central to the quantitative element of your case(s). The measurement of these attributes will consist of mapping the magnitude of these attributes to a numerical value (Lee and Lings 2008). Attributes that you may want to measure could include anything from the number of hours in a working day, the number of key strokes per minute to measurements of theoretical constructs such as attitudes, perceptions or satisfaction. In preparing your theoretical frameworks, you will have read the work of other researchers who will have conducted these measurements, so read how they carried out their measurements, how they analysed their data and how they presented their findings. You are strongly advised to study the research design of these studies in informing your own research.

Surveys

A very common example of a survey is a 'mall intercept', where shoppers are asked by a researcher in a shopping centre or mall to answer a number of set questions. Surveys therefore consist of asking people face to face, over the phone or via email to answer a structured set of questions or statements and recording their answers (Maylor and Blackmon 2005). Surveys are particularly useful in the following situations:

- You know who can answer your questions.
- You are seeking opinions, attitudes, facts or behaviours.
- You want to collect data from 20+ respondents.
- You have a clear idea of the questions that you need to ask and they are straightforward.

Surveys can capture quite simple information, for example measuring attitudes towards changes in office design, staff perceptions of changes to working hours or more complex ideas such as measuring a theoretical construct, such as job satisfaction. A common example of a survey is a self-administered questionnaire, where the respondents complete the questionnaire themselves, recoding their answers using a form of multiple-choice response, for example a range of answers from 'completely satisfied' to 'completely dissatisfied'. Questionnaires are a very common method in research, and collecting data through a self-administered questionnaire, particularly online, can be very effective. A survey is also an appropriate data collection method as part of a case study strategy which can be triangulated with, for example, interviews or observation (structured or unstructured), as well as a secondary data source. The following research insight provides an example of how a survey formed part of the data collection in a single case study.

Research insight: surveying the customers

Waheed was investigating cross-cultural marketing in a business-to-business context in a large telecoms company in the middle-east. As part of finding out about the cross-cultural marketing practices, he wanted to gather the perceptions of the business customers of the company. With this size of the organization, he was able to survey a sample of customers as a means of measuring their perceptions. His instrument was adapted from existing measures of cross-cultural marketing.

The ubiquity of questionnaires in research may lead to the erroneous impression that they are easy to design. If you are planning to use a questionnaire as part of your data collection or indeed any other form of structured survey, then allow plenty of time for preparation. You are strongly advised to adapt a questionnaire that has been published and hence met stringent research quality criteria for your research. This is all the more important in case study research where a survey is likely to form only one of the data sources. Do not reject the measures if they have not been used in your particular context. The strength of a good measure is its theoretical foundation which usually makes it adaptable to a range of situations. Creating and refining a set of items with suitable responses for a rigorous questionnaire as part of a multiple data collection strategy is probably best avoided. Examiners can get very engaged in the design of a research questionnaire and ask some very awkward questions if they feel that the questionnaire is not properly designed.

In designing your research instrument, you will have already thought about who will be able to give you the information that you need. The following section is concerned with choosing and reaching your respondents.

Sampling

In Chapter 3, sampling focused on choice of cases, for example the selection of companies or teams as units of analysis in the research strategy. In this chapter, sampling deals with the selection of respondents who can provide the answers to a quantitative research instrument. The starting point for your sampling is to clarify the population of your study. Population refers to the whole set of entities, as illustrated in the following research insight.

> ### Research insight: populations and samples in case study research
>
> Louella was studying paternity leave within the context of professional services. She had been able to negotiate access to four providers of these services that included accounting, surveying and legal services. She had chosen a survey to measure attitudes so she had to define the population for her survey. Did she just choose male respondents or include female ones too? Did she include part-time as well as full-time staff? Having decided that female responses were just as important for her research as male, her population was going to consist of *all* staff on the payrolls of the participating organizations, whether they had taken paternity leave or not. She then worked out the size of the sample that she needed for her statistical analyses, which included some thoughts about her likely response rate. She then had to consider how she was going to distribute her questionnaire and how she could maximize her response rate.

The aim of rigorous sampling is to achieve representativeness and precision (Easterby-Smith et al. 2008). In case study research, therefore, examples of populations could be all employees, all managers or all clients within the units of analysis. When pursuing a multiple case study design, the populations should share the same characteristics across all cases. The researcher will have to appreciate the difference between probability and non-probability sampling (see, for example, Saunders et al. 2007) but, effectively, non-probability sampling will usually suffice for a survey in case study research. Common examples of non-probability sampling are judgement, purposive and convenience (Easterby-Smith et al. 2008) or quota and your choice will depend on your research objectives and practical issues. A critical question is how large your sample should be. Sadly, there is no definitive answer other than it depends on what you are trying to achieve. A discussion with your supervisor(s) is very valuable in this matter, bearing in mind that a large sample may not necessarily fulfil what you are trying to achieve. The reader/examiner will want to be reassured that the sampling procedure in your research was carried out in accordance with accepted protocols (see Further reading); they will want to see an explanation of what you did, supported by references to recognized sources. They do *not* want to see a discussion of possible sampling options with no clear explanation of what you actually did and the bases for your decision making.

What do you want to know?

At the same time as establishing who is likely to have the answers to your questions and the size of the sample you need, you will be thinking of how you are going to obtain the answers to the questions. Remember that quantitative data are concerned with measurement so double check that you are very clear about what you are aiming to measure and how this measurement is contributing to the research objectives of the case study research strategy. As with the design of the research instruments, you are advised to look at the methods sections of research papers to see what sampling procedures the authors have used. You will also be able to see the size of samples which the reviewers of the papers have deemed acceptable. As a case study researcher, you will need to remember that you are not making the same claims about your quantitative data as a research study based entirely on survey data.

Getting responses

A great deal of work has to go into creating the research instrument for a survey, which in many instances is a structured questionnaire. You usually have only one opportunity to gather these data and therefore you should aim to 'get it right first time', which will involve seeing whether your instrument will work. You are advised to test your instrument, first in a pre-test with informed colleagues and then through a pilot with a small sample of the population of interest. This phase in the preparation will enable you to check that your questions are intelligible, that you are getting the sort of answers that you need and that the instrument is not going to be too time-consuming for respondents to complete. It is clearly vital for your research that your sample is going to respond in sufficient numbers for you to achieve an acceptable response rate. In selecting how the respondents are going to complete the questionnaire, you will have to abide by research ethics procedures and the access agreements that you have made with your participating cases. Electronic distribution of the questionnaire assists greatly in this method of data collection but it still requires people to give up their time to supply the answers. Do not forget to think about the costs that your respondents will incur in participating in your research. Detailed guidance about obtaining responses to structured research instruments is available in the Further reading section.

Qualitative data

A great many case studies feature qualitative data as they are well suited to in-depth investigations. Mason (2002) insists that the researcher conducts qualitative research at a strategic level, while at the same time remaining flexible and contextual. This maxim can be understood to refer to the careful planning and preparation of interview guides and informant selection but equally to responding to changing situations and being alert to adapting research to new material and/or theory. The following research insight describes a well-honed means of generating qualitative data.

Research insight: focus groups

Queuing on the phone to get through to a utility company or financial services institution seems to be a way of life. Mohammed thought that it would be valuable to discover what call centre operatives thought about keeping customers on hold in terms of job satisfaction and hence retention. Luckily, he was able to persuade a large company to act as a case and to allow him to talk to call centre operatives. Focus groups were chosen as a means of generating material for one source of data. Two focus groups of eight call centre operatives were put together. Focus group participants were provided with ethical consent forms with further verbal assurances that their responses would be anonymous, although the discussions were recorded. The focus group participants were asked a series of questions from a guide that Mohammed had prepared in advance which encouraged them to talk in a relaxed manner about their jobs. The guide also provided the means for keeping the focus group discussions more or less on track.

No matter what particular data collection technique you are planning to use as part of the overall data collection for your case study, as always, careful preparation is essential. Case study research lends itself to a research approach known as ethnography, which implies some close involvement with an organization or group (Easterby-Smith et al. 2008), or tribe as is common in anthropology (Remenyi et al. 1998). Data can be generated through observation where the researcher can be part of the organization for the duration of the research as participant-observer. In ethnographic studies, the overall approach to data collection may be a little less structured than in realist or post-positivist studies and may consist of a number of different data sets such as interviews, diaries, notes of observations and video recordings. We will concentrate on interviews and observation in this overview of qualitative data collection.

Interviews

In qualitative data collection, interviews are usually semi-structured (see Figure 5.2), which means that they follow an interview guide but allow for the flexibility and contextual adaptation that Mason (2002) requires. The following basic elements for preparing a semi-structured interview guide have been proposed:

- Without sounding too obvious, do make sure that the questions you ask relate to your research objectives.
- Be sure to adhere to ethical research principles, which will assist in creating a situation where you are trusted. Your behaviour after the interview will also contribute to the interviews that follow, that is, to be discrete and respectful to your informants.
- Create an order in your interview guide so that the questions follow logically. Allow space for 'probing' or returning to an answer that needs further attention.
- Use language that is comprehensible and familiar to the informants. Ask them to explain any unfamiliar terms that they use. You may wish to arrange an interview on neutral ground in this case. Interviewing a senior manager in their office may be a bit intimidating and practically there may be interruptions.

- Make sure that you keep scrupulous records of who (including detail of position, how long they have worked for the company and how long they have been in that job), when, where, how long.
- Jot down some thoughts immediately after each interview, capturing the 'highlights'. These notes are known as an *aide-mémoire* and act as a preliminary means of analysis. (Compiled from Bryman 2001 and Easterby-Smith et al. 2008)

Interviews can be face to face, via the telephone or using any other means such as 'chatrooms', Skype etc. The role of the interviewer is to create a situation that encourages the informant to talk about the subject of the research. The ability to listen and simultaneously keep the 'conversation' going along the lines that the researcher requires is an advanced skill. Listen to some of the interviewers on good news programmes – for example, Jon Snow on Channel 4 in the UK is particularly good. If you have conducted your ethical processes within your cases, then you may have gone some way to establishing levels of trust that are so important in conducting good interviews (Easterby-Smith et al. 2008). Discretion about the data collected in the interviews and respect for your informants are essential for ethical research. This is all the more important when you are immersed in the case as opposed to interviewers who just visit an organization once to collect data. It is expected that interviews are recorded and that full transcripts of the interviews are made. There may be some informants who decline to be recorded. If this is the case, then you, as a researcher, have to consider the implications of collecting data that some readers/examiners may question. You are not going to be able to note down the whole interview and ask questions at the same time. You may want to 'ask a friend' to help you with these interviews where you ask the questions and your friend makes as full a record of the interview as possible.

Selection

The informants for your interviews, just as the respondents for a survey, need to be able to provide the information that you require. Interpretivist researchers may avoid the term 'sampling' but a process of selection nonetheless takes place. The selection will depend upon the information that you seek but your participants will be selected because you think that they will provide an important perspective that will elucidate and clarify aspects of the investigation (Polkinghorne 2005). In this research insight, the decisions about who to interview seem to have been driven by obtaining a range of experiences from different firms, age groups, genders and positions, and which could be described as maximum variation or selection (Creswell 2007).

Research insight: career plateau

Smith-Ruig (2009) used semi-structured interviews to gather data on the feelings, attitudes and motivations of informants in the accounting profession to provide a very individualized account of their career development. She conducted 59 interviews and, in the paper, she provides information about the informants in terms of age, position by gender in the accounting firms, the type of firms that the informants worked for, as well as positions in the corporate and university sector such as associate professor or manager. The participants were selected by means of purposive, convenience and snowball sampling with 30 men and 29 women being interviewed.

Students ask the same questions in qualitative research as in quantitative research in regard to the number of respondents/informants that are needed for their research. In qualitative research, it is even less easy to arrive at a number. Since the objective of qualitative research is generally to understand, usually fewer informants are needed – in fact, the 59 informants cited in the research insight is a large selection. For a case study researcher, the number could be lower without necessarily having a negative impact on the research. Sampling approaches for qualitative data collection might include (Creswell 2007):

- Snowball: where informants are identified by people who know others who are appropriate for being able to provide the desired information.
- Opportunistic: where new leads are suggested from unexpected sources.
- Politically important: appropriate in case study research where some people have to be interviewed.

What is important is that you create an argument in your dissertation or thesis that supports who you interview and why they were chosen. In case study research, you have already selected your site, therefore to some extent the choice of your informants is already narrowed. You must still provide an explanation of how your informants were selected and what sort of sampling procedures formed the basis of the selection.

Observation

Observing the behaviour of people often addresses some of the bias that may influence the way in which they answer questions. According to Bryman (2001), interview informants may have an inaccurate recall of events, or their responses may be influenced by social desirability, rendering their information less credible. Observation can, therefore, provide a means of triangulating interview material (Polkinghorne 2005). The following research insight provides an example of semi-structured observation.

Research insight: detail in retail

Retail establishments have clearly defined procedures for responding to customer enquiries but when a customer makes a complaint aggressively, sometimes these procedures are not adhered to. Benjamin was conducting a comparative case study in two large retailers, studying how staff coped with customer complaints. He piloted a semi-structured instrument from the complaint literature that consisted of 10 staff behaviours that formed the basis for observations. After discussion with his supervisors and the participating retailers, he made some refinements to his research instruments and then embarked on the data collection. He spent many hours observing staff behaviours in complaining situations across the two cases. He soon discovered that prime times for complaints were weekends and lunchtimes. He therefore concentrated his data collection to coincide with these busy periods but still covered some of the slower times to ensure variation in his data collection.

Observation, as shown in Figure 5.2, is suitable for the collection of quantitative as well as qualitative data in this section. In this section, we will review observation within the tradition of ethnography. Ethnography is a type of research that involves substantial immersion in a group of interest such as a tribe, often over a period of years. Ethnographic research covers a number of data collection techniques but observation as a participant or tribal member is common. This approach is also used in business and management research as it allows for deep understanding of organizational culture (Remenyi et al. 1998). Although your investigation may not take place over a period of years, you may find that participant observation as a technique could add considerable insight into your research question/problem. Preparation for observation data collection is as important as any other data collection technique. As illustrated in the research insight above, the development of an instrument for collecting data using observation is essential. Table 5.3 provides an example of a participant observation guide that can be adapted to suit a number of research problems/questions.

Participant observation data can be collected in chunks of time, during periods of activity that relate to the research question or other periods that capture the appropriate data as shown in the research insight. You will need to provide an explanation of what you observed, why you observed it and when you observed it in your dissertation or thesis. Much observation data are collected by means of notes but the ubiquity of digital images provides the researcher with alternatives for data capture.

Table 5.3   Participant observation

Category	Includes	Researchers should note
Appearance	Clothing, age, gender appearance	Anything that might indicate membership in groups of interest to the study, e.g. profession, social status, status in the organization or holding influence or power
Verbal behaviour and interactions	Who speaks to whom and for how long, who initiates the interaction, tone of voice	Gender, age, ethnicity, profession, dynamics of interaction
Physical behaviour and gestures	What people do, who interacts with whom, who is not interacting	How people use their bodies and voices to communicate different emotions, what individuals' behaviours indicate about their feelings towards one another, rank or function in the case
Personal space	How close people stand to each other	What individuals' preferences concerning personal space suggest about their relationships
Human traffic	People who enter, leave and spend time at the observation site	Where people enter and exit, how long they stay, who they are (ethnicity, age, gender), whether they are alone or accompanied
People who stand out	Identification of people who receive a lot of attention from others	Characteristics of these individuals, what differentiates them, whether people consult them or whether they approach other people, whether they seem to be strangers or well known by others present

Adapted from Qualitative Research Methods: A Data Collector's Field Guide (www.fhi.org/nr/rdonlyres/.../participantobservation1.pdf)

Before getting too carried away with capturing lots of visual images, you need to think very carefully about how these images are going to be analysed and presented. In all qualitative data collection, making short notes immediately after the collection of the data will assist in the subsequent analysis. Since you are going to be triangulating your observation data with text-based data, you should work out in advance how you will bring all the data sets together.

An important feature of qualitative research is the element of researcher self-scrutiny or reflexivity (Mason 2002) which refers to taking account of what has been done. As researcher subjectivity is embedded in qualitative research, a critical evaluation of the researcher role in the research should enable a more reasoned and credible outcome. This is doubly true in case study research where immersion not only in the data but also in the situation calls for a particularly incisive perspective on the researcher stance. This discussion is an overview of primary data collection techniques that lend themselves to case study research. You will have to consult specialist literature on all these techniques and others that might also be appropriate for your investigation. Please remember that reading academic papers will provide examples of good research method practice for further guidance in collecting primary data. The following research insight illustrates how a researcher brought together data sources and techniques in a single case study.

Research insight: mixing the methods

Eloise was investigating the impact of films on tourism, specifically through a single case study of New Zealand. Her research objectives were concerned with exploring consumer decision making in selecting destinations and looking for growth in visitor numbers. She mapped out her data sources in line with these research objectives. Her primary data collection consisted of two sets of in-depth interviews. First, she interviewed an international selection of tourists whose decisions were influenced by seeing *Lord of the Rings*. The second set of interviews was arranged with tourism managers who had made use of the film's location in their marketing communications. In addition to her interview material, her secondary data were obtained by analysing quantitative data in government publications on tourism growth, specialist tourist reports and practitioner publications, focusing mainly on growth statistics.

The discussion now moves on to secondary data sources for case study research.

Secondary data

Use of secondary data tends to vary across the disciplines in business and management. In marketing, analysis of these data is not at all common in research papers, whereas in finance and economics, it forms a pivotal source for research. The need for triangulation in case study research provides an excellent opportunity for using this under-valued data source. You must apply the same principles of rigour to the secondary data that you do to primary data. It is noticeable that students do not view their secondary data sources in the same way as primary data. The reader/examiner needs to be assured of the credibility and quality of secondary data just as much as primary data.

The source of secondary data in case study research may be from the case itself, such as minutes of meetings or websites (internal and external). External data sources may also be relevant from sources such as government information or privately generated market data from companies like Mintel. The following research insight provides an example of using secondary data from two different sources in a study into good governance codes (Zattoni and Cuomo 2010).

Research insight: non-executive directors

The researchers obtained data on codes of good governance in 60 countries from EU and OECD publications, concentrating only on codes of good corporate governance in their investigation into the incentivization and competence of non-executive directors. Countries were classified according to legal tradition, membership of EU and their board model. They assigned codes of 1 or 0 to the countries, according to their conceptual framework. They then collected archival data on the content of the governance codes, again assigning 1 or 0 to measure the presence of key characteristics in the conceptual framework. The assigning of quantitative codes to qualitative data enabled them to match the two data sets (codes of good governance and content of codes). Their study concluded that good governance codes encourage boards to increase the number of non-executive and independent directors.

This study is based entirely on secondary data but is a good example of how to exploit secondary data. By assigning quantitative codes to qualitative secondary data, the authors optimized data sources to enable them to make their contribution to knowledge. You do not necessarily have to manipulate secondary data as they may already be in a form that you can use quite readily for your research. Table 5.4 summarizes the key advantages and disadvantages of secondary data.

There are key steps in evaluating secondary data (Saunders et al. 2007). First, you need to assess the overall suitability of the data to your research objectives. Do the existing data generate the measures that you need? If you are interested in customer satisfaction data, are these data captured in a form that you intend to manipulate, e.g. Likert-style responses? Similarly, you need to be aware of bias that is likely to be encountered in reports, minutes and other in-house documentation. The credibility of the data is the second means of evaluation. To some extent, 'brands' work well here, with such organizations as Ipsos or Office of National Statistics being trustworthy sources. For in-house reports, you will have to check carefully on how these data are collected, by whom and what checks there are for validity and reliability. The final aspect of evaluating secondary data is the costs and benefits not only involved in accessing the data but in carrying out the manipulations and evaluations.

You can approach secondary data from two distinct stances. The most straightforward stance is where the data are used without any further processing or manipulation but with careful attention to sources. How can you decide whether the secondary data that you are planning to access meet the standards of rigour and reliability that

Table 5.4   Secondary data in case study research

	Advantages	**Disadvantages**
Effort	Can be done from a desk (hence desk research), saving time and effort	Need to understand and get 'into' data, understanding what the researcher(s) were trying to do Expectations of high levels of analysis May have to pay for data sets
Analysis	May be very high quality data, large samples, sophisticated techniques with global or cross-cultural comparisons possible New directions from existing data sets More considered approach owing to extra time	No control over data quality Bias may be difficult to ascertain and hence account for
Contribution	Provides a basis for triangulation, longitudinal research and therefore new insight	Credibility may be questioned

Adapted from Bryman and Bell (2003) and Maylor and Blackmon (2005)

you anticipate your primary data sources will have? We have all heard about reports being condemned for weak methodologies, small sample sizes and unsound conclusions. Some of these criticisms are undoubtedly voiced by people who do not like what the report is saying and see a way to undermine the report's findings by attacking the methods. The last thing you want is someone poking holes in your secondary data sources, therefore you must spell out your sources, how they were evaluated and the analyses that you performed on these data (which we shall discuss in Chapter 6). The reader will find a summary of data sources very helpful in understanding your research. Table 5.5 shows how Stensaker and Langley (2010) presented their data sources for their comparative case study into a planned change initiative across three divisions in a large multinational company.

Before you panic at the amount of data, you will note that the study lasted for four years and was conducted by experienced researchers. You will note that the table provides a very comprehensive overview of the data in the study which contributed to the quality of the study.

It is hoped that this discussion has convinced you that careful planning of your data collection is indispensable for your case study investigation. Although the use of a number of different or dissimilar research methods increases the value of case study investigation (Woodside and Wilson 2003), there are costs incurred in learning about different research techniques and time in generating different data sets (Yin 2009). These learning costs will need to be incorporated into the timing of your research plan, but the benefits of being familiar with a range of data collection techniques is of considerable advantage in academic and practitioner professions. In the next section, we consider how the various data sets can be brought together in the process of triangulation.

Table 5.5 An example of presenting data sources

	Interviews	Observation	Archival data	Timing of collection
Corporate level	6	7	10	Jan 1998 to Dec 2001
Division 1	26	22	11	Contact established in autumn 1998
Top managers and change agents	9			Intensive data collection Jan to Sept 1999
Middle managers and employees	17			Follow-up interviews until Dec 2001
Division 2	38	5	12	Contact established in spring 2000
Top managers and change agents	12			Intensive collection May to Dec 2000
Middle managers and employees	26			Follow-up interviews until Dec 2001
Division 3	14	5	10	Contact established in spring 2001
Top managers and change agents	11			Intensive data collection Jan to May 2001
Middle managers and employees	13			Follow-up interviews until Dec 2001
Total	84	39	43	Four years

Adapted from Stensaker and Langley (2010)

Triangulation

Triangulation is a key concept in case study research, especially with reference to triangulating data sources or data methods. As case study research can consist of multiple data sources or multiple methods, there is a need to bring these various sources together at some stage, which Yin (2009: 115) describes as 'converging lines of enquiry'. Using multiple methods occurs widely in research, many quantitative studies are preceded by an exploratory qualitative phase (for example, Gwinner et al. 1998) or a survey can be followed up by in-depth qualitative investigation. In purely qualitative studies, researchers may argue for the credibility and trustworthiness of their findings on the basis of triangulation (Robson 2002), such as interviews and focus groups. It is argued that if two or more sources provide similar perspectives, then they can to some extent cross-validate each other. The combination of qualitative and quantitative data into a study of the interrelationships between work perceptions and a computer information system enabled the researchers to resolve inconsistencies in their research findings (Kaplan and Duchon 1988). Like everything else in research, planning how you are going to triangulate your data is essential. Just hoping that various data sets will triangulate themselves is not going to convince the reader/examiner.

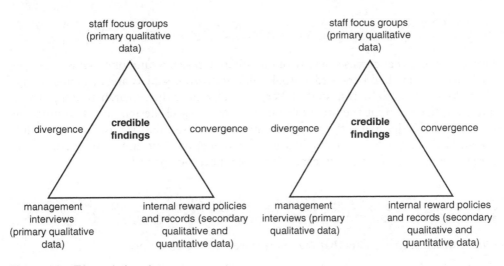

Figure 5.3   Triangulating data

When you are drawing up your data collection procedures for the case study, you will have to incorporate into the design how you will triangulate the data from each of the sources that you have accessed, as well as the cases that you have investigated. Figure 5.3 provides an illustration of mapping three data sources as triangulated in a study of two cases. As shown in Table 5.1, you should aim to have similar data sources in each case. In Figure 5.3, you will note that statements about reality or fact have been avoided and that the convergence (or divergence) of data instead provides the basis for the 'credibility' of the findings.

The analysis of the data that will form the basis for triangulation will be presented in Chapter 6.

An important concluding remark for this chapter on data collection is that more data are not necessarily better. As Figure 5.3 shows, the quantity of data increases with the more cases that you study. The reader/examiner would much rather see small but well-constructed data sets that are aligned to your research objectives. Research tends to get more complicated as you work through the process and a good maxim is to try it keep it all as simple as possible. Sprawling data sets are likely to cause problems in analysis and interpretation.

Summary

- Case study research consists of multiple sources of data or evidence but more is not necessarily better.
- These data can be primary and/or secondary and qualitative and/or quantitative but must be consistent across the cases.
- Data sources need to be chosen systematically and in accordance with research objectives.
- Data analysis needs to be planned at the same time as data gathering, whether quantitative or qualitative.
- Triangulation is a means of establishing credibility in your case study research findings and how the data are going to be triangulated is part of the data-gathering process.

Exercises

Find *one* paper that consists mainly of quantitative research and *one* that is based on qualitative data in highly ranked journals relevant to your subject area, e.g. marketing. They do not need to be case studies. Very carefully, note the research aim/objectives/ question, the way that the literature informs the research design and then note the method of eliciting data, the way the data are analysed and the contribution that the author(s) argue for. You should see a clearly mapped out and entirely consistent thread running through the research. If you cannot, look again!

Key words

Quantitative data are data that invite measurement or counting.

Qualitative data are data that invite understanding or interpretation.

Sampling (statistical) allows researchers to draw conclusions about the units of study from a sub-set of the population of interest.

Further reading

Creswell, J. W. (2007) *Qualitative Enquiry and Research Design: Choosing Among Five Approaches*, Thousand Oaks, CA: Sage Publications.
Davies, M. (2007) *Doing a Successful Research Project: Using Qualitative or Quantitative Methods*, Basingstoke: Palgrave Macmillan.
Easterby-Smith, M., Thorpe, R. and Jackson, P. (2008) *Management Research* (3rd edition), London: Sage Publications.
Lee, N. and Lings, I. (2008) *Doing Business Research: A Guide to Theory and Practice*, London: Sage Publications.

References

Bryman, A. (2001) *Social Research Methods*, New York: Oxford University Press.
Bryman, A. and Bell, E. (2003) *Business Research Methods*. Oxford: Oxford University Press.
Creswell, J. W. (2007) *Qualitative Enquiry and Research Design: Choosing Among Five Approaches*, Thousand Oaks, CA: Sage Publications.
Dooley, L. (2002) 'Case study research and theory building', *Advances in Developing Human Resources*, 4, 335–354.
Easterby-Smith, M., Thorpe, R. and Jackson, P. (2008) *Management Research* (3rd edition), London: Sage Publications.
Easton, G. (2010) 'Critical realism in case study research', *Industrial Marketing Management*, 39, 1, 118–128.
Gwinner, K. P., Gremler, D. D., Bitner, M. J. (1998) 'Relational benefits in service industries: the customer's perspective', *Journal of the Academy of Marketing Science*, 26, 2, 101–114.
Kaplan, B. and Duchon, D. (1988) 'Combining qualitative and quantitative methods in information systems research: a case study', *MIS Quarterly*, 12, 4, 571–586.
Lee, N. and Lings, I. (2008) *Doing Business Research: A Guide to Theory and Practice*, London: Sage Publications.

Mason, J. (2002) *Qualitative Researching* (2nd edition), London: Sage Publications.

Maylor, H. and Blackmon, K. (2005) *Researching Business and Management*, Basingstoke: Palgrave Macmillan.

Polkinghorne, D. (2005) 'Language and meaning: data collection in qualitative research', *Journal of Counseling Psychology*, 52, 2, 137–145.

Remenyi, D., Williams, B., Money, A. and Swartz, E. (1998) *Doing Research in Business and Management: An Introduction to Process and Method*, London: Sage Publications.

Robson, C. (2002) *Real World Research* (2nd edition), Oxford: Blackwell.

Saunders, M., Lewis, P. and Thornhill, A. (2007) *Research Methods for Business Students* (4th edition), Harlow: Pearson Education.

Smith-Ruig, T. (2009) 'Exploring career plateau as a multi-faceted phenomenon: understanding the types of career plateaux experienced by accounting professionals', *British Journal of Management*, 20, 610–622.

Stensaker, I. and Langley, A. (2010) 'Change management choices and trajectories in a multidivisional firm', *British Journal of Management*, 21, 7, 7–27.

Woodside, A. and Wilson, E. (2003) 'Case study research methods for theory building', *Journal of Business and Industrial Marketing*, 18, 6/7, 493–508.

Yin, R. (2009) *Case Study Research: Design and Methods* (4th edition), Thousand Oaks, CA: Sage Publications.

Zattoni, A. and Cuomo, F. (2010) 'How independent, competent and incentivized should non-executive directors be? An empirical investigation into good governance codes', *British Journal of Management*, 21, 63–79.

Managing and Analysing Data

6

Learning outcomes

At the end of this chapter, the reader will be able to:

- develop a strategy for analysing their data, both primary and secondary;
- present their data accessibly and attractively;
- understand how to triangulate data or methods;
- store, organize and manage data.

Introduction

This chapter sets out an overall strategy for analysing case study data so that the reader/examiner can easily comprehend the findings of your research and follow how you arrived at these findings. In addition to providing a clearly marked trail for your reader/examiner to follow, the more accessibly and attractively your research is presented the better. The reader/examiner will know that you have thought about this matter carefully and appreciate the efforts that you have put into the analysis and presentation. Yin (2009) comments that case study researchers often neglect plans for analysis and are accordingly faced with a huge amount of jumbled and possibly incoherent data. This alarming situation will not occur with you because you will have planned your study meticulously from the very beginning. Although there will have been changes – a strength of case study research is its adaptability – because you have had a plan, you will have been able to respond and capture unforeseen data collection opportunities within the overall envelope of your research. As with the previous chapter, you are strongly advised to read specialist texts on qualitative and quantitative analysis for the detail that is beyond the scope of this book. The following research insight revisits the example of the single case study initially described in the previous chapter.

Research insight: analysing the mix of data

Eloise was well under way in collecting her data for her investigation into the impact of films, in particular the Lord of the Rings, on tourism in New Zealand. Her research objectives were concerned with consumer decision making and growth in visitor numbers. She had

(Continued)

(Continued)

completed the consumer interviews and, from her analysis of these data, she had been able to draw up a guide for her in-depth interviews with tourist managers. The analysis of these interviews was also under way even though there were another 10 to do. Eloise was already noticing where the data from the two samples converged, along with several incidences of divergence. On the basis of her data, she was now beginning to be able to explain part of this increase in numbers to the popularity of the film series and the actions of the tourism managers.

In this research insight, you will note that one set of interviews provided the questions for the interview guide of the managers. The mix of different types of data or methods in this research insight is fairly typical for case study research but Eloise is developing skills in interview analysis only. If a survey generating quantitative data had been used, then quantitative data analysis skills would be needed. Further skills and discipline are required in designing and maintaining detailed records of the sources, the methods used in analysis and analysis, so make a note of <u>everything</u> and have a good storage system that suits you and the investigation. You need to ensure that you:

- Can attribute every data source including date of access.
- Have ready access to all the documents that you have collected, prioritizing the most used.
- Clarify which figures and tables you have developed yourself, those which you have adapted and those that have been compiled from a number of sources with all the required information.
- Understand precisely which information relates to which case.
- Are able to manage analysis within and across data (see below).

There will be some trial and error in the way that you manage your data storage. It may also be worth making time as you progress through your study to think about how successfully your data storage system is supporting your research. If it is not working quite as well as you wish, stop and take the time out to revisit some of the particular issues that are making your study a little less of a challenge. Having thought about data storage and set up systems which you are happy with for the time being, you can then move on to analysing the data that you have collected and stored.

Quantitative analysis

The analysis of quantitative data is judged on how it contributes to the overall research question and its integration with other data sets that make up the research strategy. The same techniques equally apply to quantitative secondary data that you are using for your research. As part of your planning, you will have thought deeply about this integration and eventual triangulation and the impact that this has on decisions about analysis. The aim of quantitative analysis is to provide information about measurement, such as the number of people that agree or how strongly they agree. Counting specified units such as words can also form the basis of analysing a data set, as the following research insight of content analysis illustrates.

Research insight: content analysis

Content analysis was adopted by Geppert and Lawrence (2008) as a means of predicting firm reputation through analysis of letters sent out to shareholders. The researchers first used computer-aided analysis to yield a total word count. Second, they compiled a variety index, which is an indicator of text quality, by counting the number of different words in the text. They then tested this index as a means of assessing the credibility of the chairmen's letters to shareholders. A high variety score is associated with apprehension or caution whereas a low score suggests a relaxation and hence truthfulness. The same software also produced five verbal themes, such as 'certainty', each with a number of sub-categories. The same data set in this instance was able to generate both quantitative measures and qualitative themes.

Two sets of analysis, as described in this research, can also serve as the basis for triangulating data. You may like to think about how a particular data set might lend itself to more than one style of analysis.

Capturing data

Your raw data could have been captured in a number of different formats. In case study research, observation data may balance interview data. If using observation, you may have collected in your data as pictures, words and numbers or a combination of all of these. In quantitative research, these observations will have been recorded in a format that will permit measurement. Table 6.1 provides an example of a structured observation guide.

Table 6.1   A form for structured observation in a retail store

Observation number:

1 Sex of shopper:
   Male
   Female

2 Approximate age of shopper:
   18–30
   31–45
   46–65
   Over 65

3 Number of individuals accompanying shopper (if none, continue to Q4):
   Number of adults
   Number of children

4 How long does the shopper stop in front of the display?
   Less than 30 seconds
   Between 30 and 60 seconds
   Over 60 seconds

5 Does the shopper handle any of the display products? Yes/no

6 How many products do they handle?
   1
   2–3
   More than 3

For each shopper and their group, a new form is completed. At the end of the data collection session, the researcher then enters the data onto a spreadsheet. Once entered, the data can then be analysed so that the research objectives are addressed. The guide will have been tested to make sure that it can be completed easily. In choosing your data collection method, you will have made plans at the same time about organizing and analysing these data.

The first step in any analysis is to put the data into the format that you need to carry out the procedures of measurement that you have planned. This process often involves entering the data from questionnaires into an electronic spreadsheet. There seems little reason for not using electronic spreadsheets, even for small data sets. Even if you have planned a fairly basic analysis involving tabulation, you may find, as the analysis progresses, that you want to use slightly more advanced techniques, which a programme such as Excel or SPSS will allow you to do. Whatever you decide to do, you will need to enter your data into the programme. This can be a tedious job but it does allow you to get an invaluable sense of the patterns in the data which is a preliminary form of analysis. Your planning will have covered key questions, such as the variables that you are measuring, how you are measuring them and how you will record the measures (Maylor and Blackmon 2005).

Quantitative coding

Data require coding, which is a process that involves assigning a numerical code to represent each possible response. One of the most common ways of recording responses to questions is 'yes' or 'no', and these responses are often coded as 1 or 2 (see Table 6.1). Other examples could include 'yes', 'no' or 'not sure', in which case the number 3 would be the code for 'not sure'. These data are known as categorical data. There are codes too for missing data and most analysis programmes will assign a code accordingly. Sadly, not all respondents complete forms fully, therefore there are always some forms which are unusable and have to be discarded. It is recommended that, just as you have consulted research papers for items for questionnaires or guides, you also emulate the analysis and coding that published researchers have used. Using existing measures is strongly recommended in any research conducted by students but particularly so in case study research where time with different data sets has to be tightly managed.

Exploring quantitative data

As you enter the data onto your spreadsheet, you are beginning to undertake preliminary analysis. The first stage of analysis is exploration and, by the time you have entered all the data, you will have some feel for the patterns that are emerging. Although this feeling is important in any research, it seems particularly important in case study research where you will be drawing together different data sets. If you have a picture in your mind of what the quantitative data are telling you, you will be able to think about what the other data sources may yield. Start thinking too, if you have not already done so, about how you are going to present your quantitative data. Again, you will find it helpful to see how experienced researchers have done this. Your reader/examiner will want to see easily how the data relate to your research objectives and how they converge with or diverge from the other data sets in the study. Look out for examples in academic papers as well as in practitioner publications, advertising and newspapers. Some analysis programmes really do not generate the results of analysis in a form that is suitable for your dissertation or thesis, so consider options of how you can make these data attractive and interesting. You can add considerable value to your findings by presenting your data thoughtfully. (We will return to this in Chapter 8.)

Describing your data

Whatever data analysis you eventually plan to carry out, it is advisable to start with the basics such as frequencies, which involves computing a frequency score for each response to a question or item. This simple process allows you to see patterns in the data and involves measures such as those of central tendency and of dispersion.

Looking for relationships

Analysis of data is often conducted on the basis of testing for the relationship between one variable and another. This is done by testing for significance, that is, the likelihood of the relationship occurring by chance alone. The procedures for testing for these relationships are governed by assumptions about your data. There is no substitute at this stage for thoroughly immersing yourself in the relevant texts, and details of these are provided at the end of the chapter. The following is an example of a common quantifiable exercise looking at associations between variables.

Research insight: measurement

Mathias was investigating post-purchase behaviour of air travellers as part of a study into the measurement of customer satisfaction within an airline. He developed five items to measure behaviour as follows:

- I will use this airline more frequently.
- I will recommend this airline to others.
- I would consider this airline as my first choice.
- I will say favourable things about this airline to others.
- I will be a loyal customer of this airline.

Each item was measured on a 7-item scale that ranged from 'definitely will' to 'definitely will not'. Mathias was able to obtain data from a convenience sample of 223 airline travellers and entered for each respondent a value between 1 and 7 for each of the items on his spreadsheet. He was able to perform an analysis that allowed him to look for associations within the data using correlation analysis.

Quantitative data are not used in case studies as extensively as they might be. This omission has led to a view that case study research consists of qualitative data. This need not be the situation and indeed the critical realist approach to case study research would lead to expectations of a quantitative study. The following research insight describes an international case study where an existing measure was used to generate quantitative data.

Research insight: organizational commitment

Baird (2004) used an existing scale (measurement of a concept) for organizational commitment as part of a case study investigation into comparing management strategies in brown field and green field sites in the USA and Australia. She argues for the use of this particular measure of organizational commitment over other measures, preferring this particular one owing to its pre-eminence in commitment research. The author states that the quantitative research augmented the qualitative analysis.

This research insight provides a good example of where an existing measure or scale was used as part of collecting data in a comparative case study investigation. Using an existing scale will also guide you to what techniques have been used by researchers who have also used this measure, how they have presented their data and what sort of conclusions they have been able to draw. A measure does not have to have been used in case study research but that does not diminish its effectiveness. What is important is that the scale's validity and reliability have been previously established.

Quantitative secondary data analysis

You may have chosen secondary quantitative data to form part of your data collection. As mentioned earlier, secondary data are not used widely enough in business research. In case study research, the use of secondary data offers a resource-friendly way of collecting data that will enable triangulation. You may be able to extract data without conducting any statistical analysis but you may also choose to derive measures by aggregating data or presenting the data in percentages rather than absolute amounts (Easterby-Smith et al. 2008), as illustrated in the following research insight.

Research insight: women's presence on the board and company performance

Although not a case study, Haslam et al.'s study (2010) provides a good example of an archival examination (secondary data) of performance data of UK FTSE companies and the presence of women on the boards of these companies from 2001 to 2005. The performance of the companies was calculated as shown in the following table, where they present the data sources and the calculations that they used on the data.

Table 6.2   Formulae for calculating company performance

Performance measure	Type of measure	Calculation
ROA (return on assets)	Accounting-based	(Earnings before extraordinary income and preferred dividend in financial year t)/(average of book values of total assets at the beginning of and at the end of the financial year t)

(Continued)

(Continued)

Performance measure	Type of measure	Calculation
ROE (return on expenditure)	Accounting-based	(Earnings before extraordinary income and preferred dividend in financial year t)/(average of book values of common equity at the beginning of and at the end of the financial year t)
Tobin's Q	Stock-based	Year-end market capitalization + average of book values of total debt at the beginning and end of the financial year t)/(average of book values of total assets at the beginning and at the end of the financial year t)

The analysis of these data provided the researchers with the company performance data that they then went on to analyse with other archival data on board composition and company characteristics, such as size of board or number of employees.

Analysis of secondary quantitative data, rather like qualitative data, is going to be largely a question of defining the criteria for selection. You can decide these criteria, as always, on the basis of addressing your research objectives and also in complementing your primary data. It is recommended that you create a research instrument for your secondary data analysis, just as you have done for your primary. As well as assisting you in working through what could be a lot of information, it is further evidence to your reader/examiner of the rigour of your research.

Qualitative analysis

A key distinction between the analysis of quantitative and qualitative data is when the analysis actually starts. Qualitative data analysis can start immediately you start collecting your data, whereas you complete your data collection before analysis in quantitative research. If you are conducting a semi-structured interview, it is common practice to make short notes about the interview immediately afterwards. Even though the data are probably not yet in a format for the main analysis, researchers will start to reflect on what the informants have said and sometimes not said. This preliminary analysis can also influence subsequent data collection in revising the research instrument or guide. The following research insight illustrates management interviews in financial services.

Research insight: the aide-memoire

Xanthe was investigating managerial decision making in customer segmentation in financial services. She had been able to select five organizations which were willing to support her research. As part of her data collection, she had organized interviews with

(Continued)

(Continued)

senior managers. All informants had been provided with an overview of the research, a letter outlining the research ethics approved by the university and a copy of the interview guide. Each interview lasted for about an hour, covering the points in the guide and probing on additional material that emerged during the course of the interviews. After each interview, Xanthe returned to her car and immediately wrote down the salient points and impressions. These notes then enabled her to approach her analysis from a new perspective.

The approaches of qualitative data analysis that are outlined below can also apply to secondary qualitative data sources. As Patton (1999) acknowledges, the multiplicity of approaches that contribute to qualitative enquiry mean that issues relating to the credibility and quality of the data are going to depend upon the audience. Basic guidelines that you may want to keep in mind have been suggested as follows:

Traceable: you must be able to show where the data have come from, who said what and which organization they come from, using recognized techniques.

Reliable: your recordings and transcripts must faithfully record the discussions or observations. Data must always be written down within 24 hours.

Complete: you must keep all your notes, recordings and transcripts in line with ethical guidelines. (Maylor and Blackmon 2005)

When writing up your research, you should include an account of the steps you took in conducting all the stages of the data collection and analysis. This is sometimes referred to as an audit trail. Qualitative research tends to yield a lot of data, for example an interview of an hour can produce 12 pages of single-spaced transcript, which has to then be multiplied by the number of interviews! By providing a record of how the data were collected, managed and analysed, you will take care of some of the criticisms that are levelled at qualitative data. In practical terms, how can substantial amounts of qualitative data be managed?

Manual or computer-driven analysis?

Many students get rather excited about the prospect of using computer-aided analysis for their qualitative data. Instead of pages of (on- or off-screen) data to code and analyse, the prospect of just pressing a few keys, as in the way that quantitative researchers appear to do, is a delight. The sad truth is that whilst using one of the many packages available for qualitative data analysis does provide some benefits, these packages do not actually analyse the data for you. The capabilities of these packages are in managing and facilitating the recursive and iterative processes that make up this sort of analysis. The more data you have, the advantages of computer-aided analysis increase. If you have smaller data sets and if you have captured data in different formats, then using NVivo or its equivalents may *not* be the solution. It is also much better for you to understand how qualitative data analysis is actually achieved manually, as you will be able to talk much more convincingly about your research if you fully grasp the processes. You also have to factor into your timetable the learning time for using what may be a new package and again this investment may not be worthwhile for a relatively small data set.

There are alternatives to using the computer-aided packages. You can, for example, use one of the word-processing packages to locate specific words or phrases in the data and find your way amongst the data, seeking words and phrases that you have identified in advance or a priori.

Getting under way

The first stage is to familiarize yourself with your data. Students consistently underestimate the time that it takes to analyse qualitative data, not appreciating the time it takes to learn and then implement new techniques and procedures, such as this familiarization process. You are most likely to transcribe your data from audio recordings and this is quite a significant undertaking. According to Saunders et al. (2007), you have four options for transcription, as follows: pay a typist to transcribe the recordings, use a transcription machine, use voice recognition software or select parts of your data to transcribe. All of these have benefits and drawbacks and ultimately you will make your own decision about transcription. The last option of selecting sections to transcribe rather goes against qualitative traditions of exploring the meaning that individuals attach to utterances and actions. This deeper understanding of data will only emerge over time, underlining the importance of allowing sufficient time to analyse qualitative data. Once the data are transcribed, Gribich (2007) recommends an initial analysis. The aim of this intial analysis is to highlight emerging issues. Once you have done this initial analysis, you can then prepare a front sheet of each interview which captures basic information, such as location, date and time, length of interview and whether there were any special circumstances relating to that particular interview. The analysis of individual interviews is sometime referred to as 'within-case'.

Analysis options

Your analysis will be driven by the style of your research and you have roughly two main options: deductive and inductive. Deductive analysis is concerned with testing the theory that you have developed for your conceptual framework. You will be looking for support for that theory in your data. For this type of analysis, you will develop codes from the theory, which are sometimes referred to as a priori codes, and develop a coding schedule. Using this schedule, you will be looking in the data for key phrases or words that support or possibly discount the theoretical frameworks that you have identified as being pertinent to your research. An advantage of this type of content analysis from a case study perspective is that it lends itself to coding that may be entered in quantitative data sets, arguably allowing for a more straightforward means of triangulation. Analysis of content therefore involves breaking down the text into manageable categories on a variety of levels, such as word, word sense, phrase, sentence or theme. The categories are then examined within your theoretical framework. You may also want to think about the relationships between the categories as suggested in the content (www.ischool.utexas.edu/~palmquis/courses/content.html).

Inductive analysis, on the other hand, is looking for emergent theoretical constructs or insights (theory generation). You will look in your data to see if there are common ideas and themes that emerge from the data and which are supported across the interviews. An example of this type of analytical approach is grounded analysis. This style of analysis seeks to uncover from the data new concepts and theories and is linked to grounded theory. Grounded analysis styles may appear more challenging because the aim is to develop a structure from the data themselves, that is, an emergent structure. With this style of analysis, build in a time for reflection (Easterby-Smith et al. 2008), where you could ask yourself how well the data are supporting or challenging existing theory.

Coding

Whatever your approach, you will have to knuckle down to the process of coding. Without coding, you will not be able to manage or interpret your data in any meaningful way. The aim is to manage the data to capture what is important with reference to your research objectives. In order to achieve this aim, you will probably have hierarchies of coding and about three levels is probably workable (see Table 6.3). Whether you have a priori codes or seek emergent codes, you will follow similar steps. The first level is to code the source of the data, for example interview with a manager (int MGR). The next level of coding can be applied to what a particular section of the interview is about, for example 'challenges' (chall). The next level of coding could be a little bit more penetrating, for example in the challenges which the manager appeared not to be coping well with (chall-nw). You should aim to land up at the third level of coding – some codes or categories capture quite large sections of data, say, 4–6 overall categories. You will have either established the name for these categories in advance or you will be seeking a name or label which is drawn from the data themselves. These

Table 6.3   An example of coding data and emerging themes

Descriptive codes	Interpretive codes	Emerging themes
admiration	other people	the role of co-shoppers
asking for and getting advice		feeling forced to buy
catwalk: negative feedback		something
catwalk: positive feedback		seeking advice
catwalk: showing off		making a joint decision?
catwalk avoidance: negative		competing with other people
feedback expected		the catwalk
deciding on my own		small talk
motivation to engage in impulse buying		
looking for reassurance after Impulse buying		
shopping with others versus. on my own		
plenty of time	time	in a hurry or on the run
quick decision making on the spot		time on my hands or window shopping
time lapse: decision now but acquisition later though ASAP		decision making on the spot
time lapse: thinking time between spotting item and impulse buy		time lapse: deciding on the spot, buying later
use: immediately after impulse buy		time lapse: time for reconsideration between decision and actual purchase
use: only some time later on		first use of the impulse purchase

Adapted from Siekmann (2009)

codes or categories are known as *in vivo*. Table 6.3 presents an example of coding used in a study of impulse purchasing by young German women. The researcher has organized her work into three types of coding: descriptive, interpretive and then the emerging themes, and represents the coding across all the interviews that she did, which as such is referred to as across-case coding. Like many researchers, the coding went through several iterations using computer-aided analysis.

In an inductive investigation, you may find that your coding will change as the analysis progresses. As described by Eisenhardt and Graebner (2007), analysis consists of a recursive cycling among the case data. It is good practice to present examples of text, codes and then themes in the tabular format shown in Table 6.2, so that the reader/examiner can see how the coding was conducted. This sort of presentation is part of the audit trail. Some of the criticisms of qualitative data are made on the basis of an apparent lack of rigour in analysis, which can in some cases be attributed to the authors not providing a detailed account of how they analysed the data. Make doubly sure that you address that potential criticism by presenting evidence of your analysis.

Qualitative secondary data

Qualitative secondary data should be subjected to similar levels of analysis as primary data. Evidence of an audit trail with secondary data must be provided. Students and sometimes more experienced researchers can overlook this audit trail which weakens their research significantly. Readers want to be assured that all the data have been subjected to accepted methods of analysis. Much of the secondary qualitative data may well be in a format that is appropriate for immediate analysis, i.e. text. If you are using recordings of conversations, speeches or images, then you will have to capture the data in a format that will support analysis. The disadvantage is that you may have to evaluate many documents and other potential data sources before getting down to actual analysis. You will need to remind yourself of your research objectives so that you can identify those data that you will select for analysis. It is as important as in primary data that you provide an account of how and why you selected your final data sources, which will obviously include an explanation of how the data allow you to achieve your research objectives. For an example of how to analyse secondary qualitative data, the following research conducted by Sonpar and Golden-Biddle (2008) provides a rigorous example of analysis following the grounded approach.

Research insight: analysis of archival data

The archival data on regionalization of health care in Alberta, Canada consisted of documents published by the government and the 17 regional health authorities. Documents that had been prepared during the sample period were examined to identify the variables of the issues that had received top managerial attention. After extensive deliberation, the variables were identified as wellness, efficiency, quality and patient satisfaction. Analyses of textual data in the documents disclosed that the issue of wellness was represented through a shift in emphasis toward keeping people healthy, as opposed to an earlier model of health care that emphasized curing disease. The issue of efficiency was represented in discussions of reducing wastages through integration of programmes, cost cutting and better use of existing resources to ensure health care costs remain under control. The quality issue was evidenced in emphasis on medical

(Continued)

(Continued)

professionalism, reduction of errors and standardization. Finally, the issue of patient satisfaction was represented through perceived quality by patients and community. The authors then go on to describe how they developed a code book to ensure consistency across the research team in coding. They describe in detail how they analysed the government reports prior to presenting their findings. Although not case study research, this research presents a rigorous example of analysing secondary data (Sonpar and Golden-Biddle 2008).

The most useful attribute that you can bring to analysis of secondary data of either type is your critical research knowledge. You should accept nothing without considering the data from all angles, such as the credibility of the source, bias that may arise and the detail given about the way in which the data were compiled. Having analysed each of the data sets, what are the implications of these data sets for the case study investigation as a whole?

Triangulation

You should have got the idea firmly in your head by now that case study research involves creating data sets from different sources, which will probably consist of different types of data. In this section, we discuss how the various data sets can be brought together in such a way that they support each other. Although the researcher is looking for convergence in the data, there is no need to panic if there is some divergence too.

When each data set has been analysed following the protocols that are appropriate for that data set, the findings of these data sets need to be brought together to enable a holistic evaluation of the data for your case study research. Even before the analyses of the different data sets are completed, you will inevitably have begun to notice patterns, themes, inconsistencies and other aspects of interest and relevance in the data, which will form the basis for bringing all these together. It is at this stage that all the planning and preparation that you have made earlier will be of enormous benefit. It is an extremely good idea to map or plot all the steps that you will take – the audit trail again. When you have some preliminary ideas, take your courage in both hands and present these ideas to your research colleagues. Your colleagues will respond by asking questions, making comments and observations. Some of these questions may be difficult to answer and will therefore test your assumptions and your approach. Although you may not like what they say, this challenging process by your colleagues will undoubtedly result in a stronger study, owing to the refinements and adjustments that their comments and observations suggest.

Triangulation is a key principle of case study research, as we have discussed in preceding chapters. Triangulation of data takes place no matter whether you are researching single or multiple cases but the purpose remains the same, which is to strengthen research findings through providing corroborating evidence from the various sources (Creswell 2007). Although we have talked about triangulation as being common in case study research, it is not exclusive to case study research. It often appears as a means of corroborating data in other studies, for example in mixed methods. The research insight describes an example of method triangulation, which is probably one of the more common instances of triangulation.

Research insight: triangulating findings

Maria was investigating how ingredient branding was adopted as a strategy in recovering a corporate failure through a case study. She had two sets of data for her single case study: interview data from senior managers and secondary data reporting responses to marketing communications. She conducted an initial analysis of each data set using a priori codes developed from the literature. She then began to evaluate the findings from both data sets. Was there support for the a priori codes and themes in the secondary data, for example strategic relationships? There was convergence in both data sets for most of the themes. However, there wasn't support across the data sets for all of the themes, hence a further examination of the data sets was conducted and yielded a more insightful explanation and hence contribution to theory.

Do not be too concerned if the findings from the data sets or methods do not converge exactly, in fact it might be a little too 'convenient' if they did. As Jick (1979: 607) states:

> When different measures yield dissimilar results, they demand that the researcher reconcile the differences somehow. In fact divergence can often be an opportunity for enriching the explanation.

Indeed, if I was an examiner of a dissertation or thesis, I would be very surprised if there was an absence of divergence in the data sets and findings and would, therefore, be asking why this was the case. The point of case study research is to investigate a research question or problem in depth and in context, therefore a discussion about divergence in the findings can demonstrate the depth of the research and support the rationale for case study research in the first place.

Whether you are seeking emergent themes or exploring a priori ideas, thinking ahead about how you will *manage* the data throughout the process should result in a less stressful process, stronger findings and, overall, a more polished output. Figure 6.1 shows how the earlier model of triangulation is developed to reflect approaches to analysis and integration. What will drive this stage is whether you are seeking emergent themes in your data or whether you are seeking some form of corroboration with the a priori models that you developed in the conceptual part of your study. Of course, there will probably be a bit of both but one approach will dominate the other or indeed provide a better explanation of the data. Your qualitative data, for example, may have generated some interesting new insights into the phenomenon under investigation and you may have then looked for support for these new insights from secondary sources. Conversely, you may have been aiming to explore key theoretical dimensions within the case or cases, in which case you may have conducted a series of structured interviews, followed up by a survey. Either way, you have the basis for synthesizing the findings from these databases.

Underpinning this example of data integration are the principles of mixed methods research. You may not have used different methods of data generation but you will have at least two data sets to interpret. For example, you could have collected data through two surveys of different samples, that is, the same method. The purpose of case study research, as we have maintained throughout, is to generate particular insight into a research question in context. The data that you have painstakingly

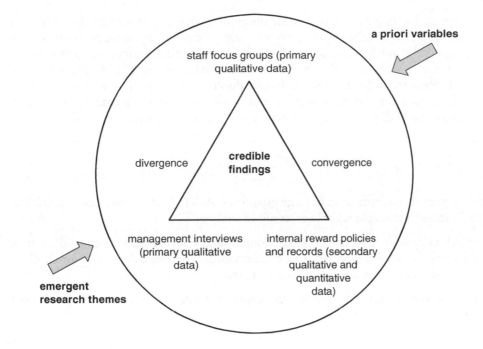

Figure 6.1   Analysis in triangulation

collected will have all been in an attempt to generate that insight and that is your starting point in pulling them all together.

The purpose of discussing triangulation at this stage is to demonstrate how the process might be conducted. In the following chapter, we will consider how to argue for the credibility of your investigation.

Summary

In this chapter, the analysis of primary and secondary data, both quantitative and qualitative, has been reviewed so that you can appreciate how various data sources are analysed separately, within case and then, if using more than one case, across case. We have considered:

- Preliminary steps in coding and analysing primary and secondary quantitative data and measurement.
- Analysing and organizing primary and secondary qualitative data.
- How various data sets of different methods can be triangulated to address the research questions and to substantiate the research.

Exercises

1   Choose five research papers in your discipline with a variety of methods. Study carefully how the data for the study were collected, analysed and presented. How many data sets are there? If more than one, what was the role played by each one? How do the data converge and/or diverge?

2 Again, looking at papers in your discipline, what appears to be the dominant research approach? If you were to adopt a case study strategy, what sort of arguments might you need to develop for making a contribution to the area?

3 Choose a news item that is current. Read, watch or listen to the reporting of this item from three to four different sources. Note the different ways in which the item is presented. Consider which source to you presents the item with most credibility and reflect on why you have arrived at this conclusion.

Key words

Coding permits the reduction of large quantities of data (quantitative and qualitative) into formats that enable reliable or credible analysis.

Content analysis focuses on the actual content and internal features of media which is used to determine the presence of certain words, concepts, themes, phrases, characters or sentences within texts or sets of texts.

Grounded analysis involves building concepts or structure from the data, teasing out themes, patterns and categories.

Further reading

Bryman, A. and Bell, E. (2003) *Business Research Methods*, Oxford: Oxford University Press.

Easterby-Smith, M., Thorpe, R. and Jackson, P. (2008) *Management Research* (3rd edition), London: Sage Publications.

Leonard-Barton, D. (1990) 'A dual methodology for case studies: synergistic use of longitudinal single site with replicated multiple sites', *Organizational Change*, 1, 3, 248–266.

Saunders, M., Lewis, P. and Thornhill, A. (2007) *Research Methods for Business Students* (4th edition), Harlow: Pearson Education.

References

Baird, M. (2004) 'Comparing cases: studies of commitment systems in Australia and the United States', *International Journal of Human Resource Management*, 15, 3, 433–444.

Creswell, J. W. (2007) *Qualitative Enquiry and Research Design: Choosing Among Five Approaches*, Thousand Oaks, CA: Sage Publications.

Easterby-Smith, M., Thorpe, R. and Jackson, P. (2008) *Management Research* (3rd edition), London: Sage Publications.

Eisenhardt, K. and Graebner, M. (2007) 'Theory building from cases: opportunities and challenges', *Academy of Management Journal*, 50, 1, 25–32.

Geppert, J. and Lawrence, J. (2008) 'Predicting firm reputation through content analysis of shareholders' letter', *Corporate Reputation Review*, 11, 4, 285–307.

Gribich, C. (2007) *Qualitative Data Analysis: An Introduction*, London: Sage Publications.

Haslam, S., Ryan, M., Kulich, C., Trojanowski, G. and Atkins, C. (2010) 'The relationship between women's presence on company boards and objective and subjective measures of company performance', *British Journal of Management*, 21, 2, 484–497.

Jick, T. (1979) 'Mixing qualitative and quantitative methods: triangulation in action', *Administrative Science Quarterly*, 24, 4, 602–611.

Maylor, H. and Blackamon, K. (2005) *Researching Business and Management*, Basingstoke: Palgrave Macmillan.

Patton, M. (1999) 'Enhancing the quality and credibility of qualitative analysis', *Health Services Research*, 34, 5, 1189–1208.

Saunders, M., Lewis, P. and Thornhill, A. (2007) *Research Methods for Business Students* (4th edition), Harlow: Pearson Education.

Siekmann, A. (2009) *Happiness and Impulse Buying*. Unpublished thesis, Oxford: Oxford Brookes University.

Sonpar, K. and Golden-Biddle, K. (2008) 'Using content analysis to elaborate adolescent theories of organization', *Organizational Research Methods*, 11, 4, 795–814.

Yin, R. (2009) *Case Study Research: Design and Methods* (4th edition), Thousand Oaks, CA: Sage Publications.

Quality in Case Study Research

Learning outcomes

At the end of this chapter, the reader will be able to:

- describe the principal characteristics of validity, reliability and generalizability in business research;
- relate alternative approaches to establishing quality in case study research;
- illustrate the key arguments for supporting research findings;
- provide a coherent argument for the quality of case study research.

Introduction

As we discussed in earlier chapters of this book, case study research attracts a great deal of criticism in establishing its credibility and hence undermines any contribution that this approach to research makes to knowledge or theory. Researchers are familiar with the term 'rigour' which reviewers use in evaluating research, which can be roughly understood as meticulousness or precision. The aim of this chapter is to ensure that your research conveys to its readers or assessors that it meets standard criteria of quality and rigour across the research domains that we have discussed in this book. We have argued so far that research of any persuasion should be based on sound research questions, solid conceptualization and research methods that adhere to established protocols and, in this chapter, we will discuss how this process should be continued with reference to arguing for the quality and contribution of the research.

You will notice that the word 'credibility' is often used in this chapter. This word has been borrowed from a number of eminent researchers, for example Glaser (1966), Patton (1999) and Lincoln and Guba (1985). Believability (Easterby-Smith et al. 2008) has also been used in this way, but the discussion will also include more familiar terms such as validity and reliability. We will also return to the vexed question of generalizability, a frequently levelled criticism of case study research.

The chapter begins with a consideration of the classical or conventional approaches to research quality.

Classical approaches to research quality

In Chapter 2 of this book, the importance of establishing an epistemological base for case study research was addressed. This theme of epistemological foundation has been reiterated throughout the following chapters. In establishing or arguing for the credibility of your research, these epistemological foundations will once again assist in demonstrating the quality of your study. If you have followed a positivist or post-positivist methodology then you would be expected to argue for the quality of your research according to the protocols for that methodology. The methods suggested by the natural science model for ensuring the rigour of your case would therefore be consistent and involve techniques such as construct validity, internal validity and reliability. Yin (2009) has helpfully adapted these criteria for case study research, suggesting that the quality of case study research is judged through the accepted tests for validity (construct, internal and external) and reliability, which are now discussed.

Construct validity

Construct validity refers to the extent to which the study investigates what it claims to investigate. Construct validity assumes an objective reality and is therefore often rejected by interpretivist researchers; nonetheless the positivist literature provides two strategies for ensuring construct validity (Gibbert and Ruigrok 2010) in case study research. First, construct validity can be argued for through triangulation (Jick 1979), that is of course using a number of data sources to minimize bias. However, triangulation alone as a means of supporting construct validity is probably insufficient. Since triangulation, according to Lee and Lings (2008), is concerned with an external reality at best, it is not clear how it can be used in isolation as a means of arguing for construct validity. The second approach for claiming a degree of construct validity is through establishing a clear chain of evidence to enable the reader to follow how the researcher went from research question to conclusion (Remenyi et al. 1998; Yin 2009). A case study where both of these approaches are evident would address some of the requirements of construct validity although not necessarily those of the hardened positivist! With closer reference to positivist traditions, however, further recommendations are to have specified ideas, concepts and relationships that form the basis of the study and to provide detail of how the measures used in the research actually addressed these ideas (Remenyi et al. 1998). If you have followed the steps that have been recommended in this book, then you should be able to argue for construct validity in your work.

In your reading, you will have looked at papers that follow positivist epistemologies and you should have noted how the researchers have constructed their measures from the theory appertaining to the concepts that they are investigating. Note the way that they have done this and ensure that you build your constructs in similar ways; you will then have gone some way to arguing for the validity of your research in this particular area.

Internal validity

Internal validity refers to the presence of causal relationships between variables and results and applies at data collection and analysis stages in research (Gibbert and Ruigrok 2010). Such considerations of internal validity usually only apply in explanatory case studies, where the researcher is trying to argue that event x led to event y (Yin 2009). More broadly, the aim of internal validity is to persuade the reader that the research findings are based on critical investigation of the data. This can be evidenced by providing detail about how the data were analysed, for example coding and within-case and cross-case analysis, which would include an explanation of how data were triangulated, that is across data types and sources (see Chapter 6). In case study research, you may be seeking to infer that event *x* did bring about situation *y*. The approach in this type of research is to try and rule out any other explanation of the causal effect. Patton (1999) suggests two ways of testing rival explanations although he is not talking explicitly about internal validity but more broadly about integrity in analysis. He says that you are not attempting to disprove alternatives but looking for data that support alternative explanations. If these alternative explanations cannot be located then greater confidence can be had in the existing explanations. This process should be articulated in the analysis phase of the research, so that the reader can be assured that this step has taken place.

A significant contributor to case study research in business and management is Eisenhardt (1989). She argues that researchers can argue for internal validity through 'enfolding the literature' (p. 544) by which she means that emerging concepts and theory from case study research need to be closely examined with the existing literature. If the findings conflict with this extant literature, the researcher needs to explore this conflict. This exploration offers opportunities for gaining even deeper insight in the research.

Reliability

Reliability refers to the absence of random error so if the research was repeated, researchers would arrive at the same insights. From a broader perspective, it is an assessment of whether the evidence is consistent and stable (Remenyi et al. 1998). Transparency and replication are key words in claims for reliability (Gibbert and Ruigrok 2010). Transparency can be demonstrated through careful documentation and references to the case study research database (Yin 2009), which also helpfully support researcher arguments for construct validity. Replication questions can be addressed through references to the planning and execution of a coherent research strategy in line with recognized protocols which would facilitate research in the future. Thought should be given to the development of tables where information about the research is presented accessibly to the reader (see, for example, Table 7.1), which demonstrate the transparency of the research.

Table 7.1   An example of establishing transparency in case study research

Type of firm	Number and relative sizes of firms included	Nature of goods or services sold
Network equipment manufacturer	One large firm	Physical goods
Telecom operator consumer outlet	Two large firms, including one dominant	Physical goods
Telecom operator business centre	Two large firms, including one dominant One large firm	Physical goods
Office supply	One large firm, one alliance of two	Physical goods
Groceries	SMEs	Physical, perishable goods
Automobile sales	One large firm, one SME	Physical goods
Bicycle retail	One large firm	Physical goods
Music retail	One large firm	Information goods
Travel planning	Two large firms, one SME	Information services

Adapted from Adelaar et al. (2004)

In this research, the authors investigated how e-commerce enhances customer value through multiple-case study research. In this table, they provide a summary of the firms that participated in the research. The reader can easily see what sort of companies participated in the research as well as the type and size of company.

Not all case study writers advocate the process of arguing for the validity and reliability of your research. Thomas (2011) declares that case study researchers do not have to worry about validity or reliability and he would probably be supported by some interpretivist researchers in this declaration. What is surprising is that he does not subscribe to standard interpretivist ways of arguing for the quality of your findings either, rejecting plausibility and credibility. Whilst his arguments are interesting, you really have to consider carefully how you are going to persuade your readers that you have done your research, case study or not, rigorously. In spite of the increase of good quality case study research, case study researchers might have to work that little bit harder than other researchers following other research approaches in arguing for the quality of their research.

Generalizability

Generalizability or, as it is sometimes referred to, external validity, relates to the belief that theories must be shown to account for phenomena not only in the setting in which they were studied but elsewhere (Gibbert and Ruigrok 2010). One of the most frequent criticisms levelled at case study research is that findings cannot be generalized according to this particular interpretation of generalizability. This criticism has created a prime obstacle in the acceptance of the contributions of case study research to business and management theory. Swanborn (2010) discusses the problem of generalization both in single and multiple case studies and defines the problem as:

> On the basis of our researched case(s), what can be said about non-researched cases?
>
> (Swanborn 2010: 66)

He queries Yin's (2009) comparison of case study research with experiments, commenting that the variables in case study research are entangled, compared with their isolation in experimental research. He concludes that generalizing from case study research is only tentatively possible (p. 71) but if case study research is to be complementary to more extensive research, the problem diminishes. Case study researchers will not find this proposition acceptable and would always assert that case study research can make a contribution in its own right.

As has been stated throughout, this standard interpretation of generalizability (statistical) is not applicable to case research where the emphasis is often on studying the phenomenon in context. In spite of this, claims have been made for statistical generalizability in case study research. It has been asserted by one author that multiple cases provide the basis for generalizability (Leonard-Barton 1990) and she states that:

> Multiple case studies on a given topic clearly have more external validity i.e. generalizability, than does a single case. (p. 258)

Nor is she alone in this belief. Johnston et al. (1999) advocate multiple-case study research throughout their contribution to the topic, proposing that generalization can be achieved through replication in multiple settings. However, the choice about whether to adopt a multiple case study approach in your study design should *not* rest on this argument of demonstrating generalizability (see Chapter 3). Case study researchers (for example, Flyvbjerg 2006; Siggelkow 2007) do not allow that multiple case studies enable any form of statistical generalization in spite of Leonard-Barton's assertion (1990). Indeed, Yin (2009) is uncompromising in his dismissal of generalizability in case study research.

> [The] analogy to samples and universes is incorrect when dealing with case studies.
> (p. 43)

From this perspective, where he likens case study research to experimental research, Yin (2009) advocates the logic of replication as opposed to the logic of sampling. The logic in this context refers to a situation where a significant finding is made in a case and a need arises to replicate the research in further experiments so that finding can be duplicated and hence considered robust. The distinction between the two is that multiple case studies in themselves do not endow your research with statistical generalizability. Multiple case studies are not the same as multiple respondents. Instead, the researcher seeks to replicate a particular finding through replicating multiple cases. Each case accordingly needs to be chosen so that it either predicts similar results or predicts contrasting results. Generalizability according to Yin (2009) is achieved through the findings being generalized to theoretical propositions, which is known as *analytic* generalization, which denotes a process where generalizing takes place from data to theory rather than to population. In analytic generalization, the findings are considered of being congruent with or connected to prior theory (Miles and Huberman 1994). The following research insight illustrates analytic generalization.

Research insight: generalizing from a single case

Frank was interested in how professional organizations were coping with the economic downturn. As a part-time MPhil student, he was able to study his own company, a specialist surveyors whose target market was the public sector. He refined his research question to how staffing decisions were made in such conditions and as such was able to generate in-depth data from a number of sources including people made redundant. As part of his literature review, he constructed a summary table of the key contributions, authors, research approaches and themes to the subject. His research approach was consistent with an in-depth single case and his primary data were qualitative. As part of his quality procedures, his discussion about the generalizability of his work was closely argued with managerial decision-making literature. His summary table made this task both easier for him and for the reader in straightforward access to the key works. His findings were therefore explicitly connected to prior theory but the value of his study was in its context of a small professional firm and the depth of the analysis.

Flyvbjerg (2006) affirms that generalization can be made from single-case study research although he considers generalization to be overvalued as a means of developing theory. He argues that the force of example is underestimated. He arrives at this conclusion after considering the black swan argument of Popper (1959), where the assertion that 'all swans are white' is falsified by the discovery of black swans. He argues that this single 'case' demonstrates that theory can be developed through the single case study. Case study research, which focuses on complex issues such as processes, structures and patterns is anti-reductionist or holistic and, as such, is not really concerned with being extended to a larger population. What is important to remember here is that multiple-case study research does *not* allow for claims of statistical generalizability. Interestingly, you will find some examples of where this has been proposed as a means of arguing for the generalizability of a study. Nonetheless, it is not advocated.

We have looked at classical approaches of judging the quality of research from a positivist or post-positivist stance. Case study research, in many instances, leans towards an interpretivist epistemology, which we move on to now.

Interpretivist views of research quality

Many interpretivist researchers believe that establishing the contribution of their study lies not in adopting positivist criteria of quality but in espousing criteria that are in tune with the epistemology of their work. If your case study research is embedded in an interpretivist epistemology then this section offers alternative but accepted criteria. Of particular relevance to the case study researcher is the stream of work from Guba and his co-author Lincoln (for example 1982, 1994). Their work is concerned with naturalistic enquiry where the research may feature a case study format and relies heavily on qualitative methods (Guba and Lincoln 1982). They develop four criteria of credibility, transferability, dependability and confirmability for establishing the trustworthiness of qualitative research and which are discussed below.

Credibility

This criterion for establishing trustworthiness can be demonstrated through the adoption of appropriate and well-recognized research methods. As argued throughout this book, readers will be more receptive to case study research conducted by students and researchers if there is clear evidence that research protocols are understood and subsequently followed. If the researcher presents background information about participating organizations, groups or data sources, this information will also assist in convincing the reader about the research. Shenton (2004) argues for including evidence of tactics to obtain honest data from informants, for example through iterative questioning in data collection dialogues. The following insight illustrates an example of building credibility in research.

Research insight: credibility

Rajeeva's study was concerned with comparing recruitment processes in SMEs. She was able to gain access to five small organizations ranging from providing cleaning services and manufacturing garments to both business-to-consumer and business-to-business companies. She decided to use secondary data consisting of HR documentation, recruitment advertisements and company websites to form one source of her data. The

(Continued)

(Continued)

primary data for the cases were generated from interviews that she conducted with HR staff about how staff were recruited into the participating case organizations. She also interviewed staff who had been through the recruitment process. To provide a means of arguing for the credibility of her research, she re-interviewed senior HR staff incorporating into her interview guide data that had emerged during the course of the earlier interviews. She also provided detail on the informants, the date and the length of interviews, how and where they were conducted, the interview guide and of course extensive information on the analysis approach adopted.

Patton (1999) discusses the enhancement of qualitative analysis through discussing its integrity and argues that this can be achieved though the testing of rival explanations. He believes that failure to find strong supporting evidence for alternative ways of presenting the data helps to increase confidence in the original explanation. This can be achieved through debriefing sessions between researcher and supervisors where interpretations have to be defended. An important conclusion is a reminder from Patton (1999) that the credibility of the researcher needs to be appreciated by the reader. It is therefore important to understand what you, as a researcher, bring to the investigation in terms of experience and perspectives. As a novice researcher, and even as a PhD student, you still fall under this heading, you are advised to incorporate a thorough explanation of your research design with references to the appropriate authors in your dissertation or thesis.

Transferability

Once more we return to a variation on the theme of generalizability or, as it is sometimes referred to in positivist terminology, external validity. The question of whether the findings of case study research can be transferred to other contexts may not be one of prime interest to the case study researcher. As we have investigated earlier (Chapter 3), a particular quality of case study research is the context in which the theory is explored or indeed developed. If you have defined or bounded your research explicitly within the appropriate theory (see Chapter 3) and argued for your case(s) as a means of advancing understanding with reference to that theory (Remenyi et al. 1998), then questions of transferability are to some extent covered. Nonetheless, as has been argued previously, you should address this particular criterion in constructing your arguments about the quality of your research. One way of arguing for transferability in interpretivist research is to provide extensive background data to establish the context of the study and detailed descriptions, which would allow readers to make their own comparisons. This kind of activity is often referred to as 'thick description' (Creswell 2007), a term which is often encountered in qualitative research. Increasingly, this kind of thick description is accompanied by detail of data sources often summarized in tabular format (see Table 7.1), endowing the research further with trustworthiness.

Dependability

According to Lincoln and Guba (1985: 299), defending the dependability of your research will involve seeking the 'means for taking into account both factors of instability and factors of phenomenal or design induced changes'. The writers mean here that a researcher may make or have to make changes in the way that they collect and analyse data for reasons that were not appreciated at the outset of the research. In research, it is acknowledged that interviewing and observing is an evolving process during which interviewers and observers acquire new insights into the phenomenon of study that can subsequently influence follow-up questions or narrow the focus for observation (Graneheim and Lundman 2004). Shenton (2004) suggests detailing the following for demonstrating the dependability of research:

1 The research design and its implementation, describing what was planned and executed on a strategic level.
2 The operational detail of data gathering, addressing the minutiae of what was done in the field.
3 Reflective appraisal of the project, evaluating the effectiveness of the process of inquiry undertaken.

If some of these approaches sound familiar, then this is because some of the 'checks' for ensuring that your research can claim credibility are very similar and tend to overlap.

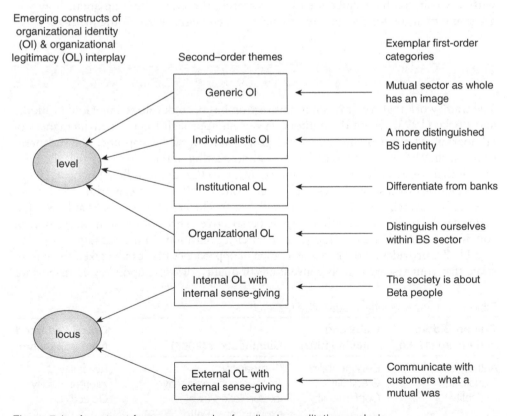

Figure 7.1   An extract from an example of coding in qualitative analysis

He and Baruch (2009)

Confirmability

In arguing for the confirmability of research, the researcher needs to persuade the reader that the research, whilst being interprevist in approach, is not overly influenced by personal values or theoretical inclinations (Bryman 2001). Please note that this is not advocating a move toward objectivity which is an anathema to the interpretivist but rather demonstrating that alternative explanations have been considered. There are familiar procedures that can be harnessed to confirm research findings, which include triangulation, an admission of researcher's beliefs and assumptions, a recognition of shortcomings in study's methods and their potential effects and, as always, detailed description of research methods, including analysis. Figure 7.1 illustrates an extract from the coding procedures in research into building societies (He and Baruch 2009).

The authors accompany this figure with detail of the grounded analysis approach that they took showing both open and axial coding (see Strauss and Corbin 1998). The reader of this paper can see how the constructs have emerged during the coding stages, thus substantiating the research through evidence of how the analysis was conducted.

The interpretivist researcher has many options open to them in terms of asserting the quality of their research. Interpretivism is a broad term that encompasses several traditions where qualitative data may be the dominant data set or method. The choice of the framework that you are going to use has to be consistent with the epistemology within which you have embedded your research, therefore thinking about how you are going to argue for the quality of your research begins early in the process.

An ethnographic contribution

The framework that we draw on in this section has been developed by Golden-Biddle and Locke (1993) where the authors set out an approach for the convincingness of ethnographic texts. Convincingness is a powerful term, which captures well the intention and the ability of the researcher in communicating to their audience that the findings of their research are worth paying attention to (Golden-Biddle and Locke 1993). Contributions to case study research often draw parallels between ethnography and case study research (for example, Creswell 2007). The next section looks at how arguments can be built from an ethnographic perspective. Three dimensions in support of convincing research are developed: authenticity, plausibility and criticality.

Table 7.2 provides an overview of a range of approaches that can be taken to demonstrate that your research meets conventions of quality, drawing upon key contributions

Table 7.2   Quality criteria in qualitative research

Golden-Biddle and Locke (1993)	Guba and Lincoln (1992)	Gummesson (2005)	Criteria adapted from positivism
Authenticity	Dependability	Comparison	Reliability
Plausibility	Credibility	Transparency alternative	Internal validity
Criticality	Confirmability	Interpretation (rival explanations, Patton 1999)	Objectivity
	Transferability	Condensing data but full reporting	Generalizability

to the area. An attempt has been made to make comparisons across the criteria but the very principles that underlie qualitative research suggest that this may be somewhat simplistic and therefore you are urged to read more extensively about quality criteria. As shown in the table, the following criteria are offered as a means of arguing the strength of your work from researchers in the interpretivist tradition.

Authenticity

According to Golden-Biddle and Locke (1993), authenticity is demonstrated in two ways: first, through portraying that the researcher was there and had sufficient experience of the case(s); second, authenticity is achieved through being genuine to the experience, that is, understanding the world of the case through abandoning their own biases and assumptions. The authors suggest authenticity can be achieved by:

- Particularizing everyday life: detail of the case(s), for example through use of quotations and illustrations.
- Providing detail on data collection and analysis: demonstration of research understanding and expertise.
- Delineating the researcher relationship with informants: how the researchers interacted with the case, including information about the length of time, their role and degree of closeness.

The question that you should address is whether the reader is being presented with an authentic portrait of what is being studied (Miles and Huberman 1994). These authors draw a parallel between authenticity and internal validity but distinguish between the measurement-oriented view of validity and instead offer such questions as 'does the study ring true and enable the reader to be there?' (p. 279).

Plausibility

Plausibility is concerned with connecting the world of the study with the readers' experience, so that the key question relating to this criterion is 'does it make sense to me'? This question implies that the study should be dealing with concerns relating to its disciplinary background but, at the same time, making a distinctive contribution to the area (Golden-Biddle and Locke 1993). The authors go on to suggest that plausibility in research can be demonstrated by the following methods:

- Normalizing unorthodox methodologies: providing familiar forms and devices establishing a connection between the study and the readers' experiences.
- Drafting the reader: where readers are invited to align themselves with the study's assertions, e.g. the use of 'we'.
- Legitimizing the atypical: writing text that attempts to shape readers' reading in such a way that they bring their own experience – for example, in business, this might be their own experience of work or consumption.
- Smoothing the contestable: reducing the likelihood of readers rejecting assertions in the study that are not in line with their experiences or knowledge. The risk of this rejection can be lessened by providing background debate to controversial assertions in the literature.

Plausibility is therefore concerned with reducing queries about the research not being in tune with the readers' own experience.

Criticality

Researchers will demonstrate that their work achieves criticality by encouraging readers to re-examine their existing ideas and beliefs. Not only is this dimension accomplished through the findings and discussion but also through form and style. Researchers need to convey their work in an appropriately animated style that engages the reader to revisit their own assumptions. Again, Golden-Biddle and Locke (1993) provide some suggestions about how criticality can be delivered:

- Carving out room to reflect: creating a break in the flow of the argument to encourage readers to stop and think.
- Provoking recognition and examination of differences: readers are encouraged to examine differences between prevailing views and the ideas articulated in the text.

These three criteria provide a means for the researcher who embraces interpretivist research to argue for the convincingness of their research. However, there is little substitute for seeing how papers published in good journals have addressed the challenges of research quality, and you are strenuously urged to have a collection of papers with methodologies that resemble your own to use as models. Readers seek to be assured that the findings of your research have been achieved through methods that they are familiar with or that are appropriate for the research design.

What works for you

You will have noticed in this chapter that, in spite of differing terminology, there seems to be considerable overlap between the actual processes suggested by authors from apparently differing and hard-to-reconcile research approaches. It is very helpful to the case study researcher in that they can use terms that embrace more than one research approach. Equally, it is helpful to be aware that some interpretivist researchers consider that to adopt what has been described here as the 'classical' tests for validity and reliability, is playing the game according to the positivist tradition, which they reject. It seems sensible therefore to consider which tradition of quality procedures you are going to choose and stick to this one and be scrupulous in the use of the relevant terminology, which comes from reading seminal papers in the field that you are studying.

If you are seeking just a quick final check, Creswell (2007) sets out the following criteria for good case study research:

- Is there clear identification of the case or cases?
- Is the case used to understand a research issue or because the case has intrinsic merit?
- Is there a clear description of the case?
- Are themes identified for the case?
- Are assertions or generalizations made from the case analysis?
- Is the researcher reflexive or self-disclosing about their position in the study?

It would not be acceptable to rely on one author for defending the credibility of your research. You need to demonstrate to the reader that you have read widely and that you understand the procedures that you have carried out.

Doctoral students should have a sound grasp of positivist procedures for arguing the quality of their work, so that work can be soundly defended on a number of fronts. Patton (1999) concludes that the important challenge for researchers, both quantitative and qualitative, is to match the methods appropriately to empirical questions and issues rather than to advocate a single method. This incisive advice returns us neatly to arguments that you will have put in place for doing case study research in the first place.

Summary

Establishing the quality of your case study research or indeed any research is axiomatic in demonstrating its contribution. This chapter has proposed a number of ways in which the case study researcher can undertake this task.

- Classical tests of quality can be applied to case study research such as internal validity and reliability.
- Generalizability in case study research is argued on the basis of analytic rather than statistical grounds.
- Case study researchers need a good understanding of a range of quality procedures from positivist, post-positivist and interpretive methodologies.
- Interpretivist approaches offer several ways of establishing the credibility of your case study work but you should be consistent.
- Questions of quality need to be thought about from the very beginning of your research.

Exercises

1 Select three papers that represent the dominant approaches in research, namely positivist, critical realist and interpretivist or an equivalent. Study carefully how the authors argue for the quality of their research and the means through which they support their argument. Make a short list of what appears to be good practice. Ask your colleagues to do something similar and compare notes.
2 Draw a series of diagrams and tables that offer opportunities for you to support your research and write an explanation. Show these to your colleagues/supervisor and ask them how easy they are to interpret and understand.

Key words

Generalizability in case study research refers to the process of considering the congruence of the findings with existing theory.

Convincingness occurs when the researcher is able to persuade the reader(s) that their work is worth taking into account on the basis of authenticity, plausibility and criticality.

Further reading

Patton, M. (1999) 'Enhancing the quality and credibility of qualitative analysis', *Health Services Research*, 34, 5, 1189–1208.
Riege, A. (2003) 'Validity and reliability tests in case study research: a literature review with "hands-on" applications for each research phase', *Qualitative Market Research*, 6, 2, 75–86.

References

Adelaar, T., Bouwman, H. and Steinfield, C. (2004) 'Enhancing customer value through click-and-mortar e-commerce: implications for geographical market reach and customer type', *Telematics and Informatics*, 21, 167–182.

Bryman, A. (2001) *Social Research Methods*, New York: Oxford University Press.

Creswell, J. W. (2007) *Qualitative Enquiry and Research Design: Choosing Among Five Approaches*, Thousand Oaks, CA: Sage Publications.

Easterby-Smith, M., Thorpe, R. and Jackson, P. (2008) *Management Research*, third edition, London: Sage Publications.

Eisenhardt, K. (1989) 'Building theories from case study research', *Academy of Management Review*, 14, 4, 532–550.

Flyvbjerg, B. (2006) 'Five misunderstandings about case study research', *Qualitative Inquiry*, 12, 2, 219–245.

Gibbert, M. and Ruigrok, W. (2010) 'The "what" and "how" of case study rigor: three strategies based on published work', *Organizational Research Methods*, 13, 4, 710–737.

Glaser, B. (1966) 'The purpose and credibility of qualitative research', *Nursing Research*, 15, 1, 56–61.

Golden-Biddle, K. and Locke, K. (1993) 'Appealing work: an investigation of how ethnographic texts convince', *Organization Science*, 4, 4, 595–616.

Graneheim, U. H. and Lundman, B. (2004) 'Qualitative content analysis in nursing research: concepts, procedures and measures to achieve trustworthiness', *Nurse Education Today*, 24, 105–112.

Guba, E. and Lincoln, Y. (1982) 'Epistemological and methodological bases of naturalistic enquiry', *Educational Technology Research and Development*, 30, 4, 233–252.

Guba, E. and Lincoln, Y. (1994) 'Competing paradigms in qualitative research', *Handbook of Qualitative Research*, Thousand Oaks, CA: Sage Publications.

Gummesson, E. (2005) 'Qualitative research in marketing', *European Journal of Marketing*, 39, 3/4, 309 –327.

He, H. and Baruch, Y. (2009) 'Organizational identity and legitimacy under major environmental changes: tale of two UK building societies', *British Journal of Management*, 21, 1, 44–62.

Jick, T. (1979) 'Mixing qualitative and quantitative methods: triangulation in action', *Administrative Science Quarterly*, 24, 4, 602–611.

Johnston, W., Leach, M. and Liu, A. (1999) 'Theory testing using case studies in business-to-business research', *Industrial Marketing Management*, 28, 201–213.

Lee, N. and Lings, I. (2008) *Doing Business Research: A Guide to Theory and Practice*, London: Sage Publications.

Leonard-Barton, D. (1990) 'A dual methodology for case studies: synergistic use of longitudinal single site with replicated multiple sites', *Organizational Change*, 1, 3, 248–266.

Lincoln, Y. S. and Guba, E. G. (1985) *Naturalistic Inquiry*, Beverly Hills, CA: Sage.

Miles, M. and Huberman, A. M. (1994) *Qualitative Data Analysis*, second edition, Thousand Oaks, CA: Sage Publications.

Patton, M. (1999) 'Enhancing the quality and credibility of qualitative analysis', *Health Services Research*, 34, 5, 1189–1208.

Popper, K. (1959) *The Logic of Scientific Discovery*, New York: Basic Books.

Remenyi, D., Williams, B., Money, A. and Swartz, E. (1998) *Doing Research in Business and Management: An Introduction to Process and Method*, London: Sage Publications.

Shenton, A. (2004) 'Strategies for ensuring trustworthiness in qualitative data projects', *Education for Information*, 22, 63–75.

Siggelkow, N. (2007) 'Persuasion with case studies', *Academy of Management Journal*, 50, 1, 20–24.

Strauss, A. and Corbin, J. (1998) *Basics of Qualitative Research: Techniques and Procedures for Developing Grounded Theory*, London: Sage Publications.

Swanborn, P. (2010) *Case Study Research: What, Why and How?* London: Sage Publications.

Thomas, G. (2011) *How to Do Your Case Study: A Guide for Students and Researchers*, London: Sage Publications.

Yin, R. (2009) *Case Study Research: Design and Methods*, fourth edition, Thousand Oaks, CA: Sage Publications.

Writing and Presenting Your Research

Learning outcomes

At the end of this chapter, the reader will be able to:

- understand the variety of presentation approaches for case study research;
- appreciate the fundamentals of presenting case study data;
- structure the case study dissertation, thesis or article to present it best;
- appreciate the benefits of working as part of a team.

Introduction

In this chapter, we will be covering the key issues of writing up your dissertation or thesis, covering such critical areas as presentation, polish and precision. Writing up is something of a misnomer as you will have been writing sections of your research from the very beginning of your investigation. You must start writing immediately – this cannot be over-emphasized – for the following reasons:

- Writing a dissertation or thesis may require a different writing style from that which you are used to. The style is formal and usually follows the conventions of your particular discipline.
- The amount of material in a dissertation or thesis is considerable. Business research theses, for example, are about 75,000–100,000 words (300 pages or so) and the sooner you begin to write and get to grips with this amount of material the better.
- What many students do not appreciate at the beginning is that once you have finished your investigation, you have to go right back to the beginning and revise the whole dissertation or thesis. However unappetizing this process may seem, it is vastly better than having to revisit notes that could have been made years ago when time has eradicated the meaning, import, significance or relevance.
- Another fundamental principle of research is that whatever you are planning to do will take you longer than you thought, so always allow more time than seems strictly necessary. The very last thing that you want to do is submit anything less than a *perfectly* polished dissertation or thesis.
- It is probably worth writing too much to start with. Generally, it is easier to reduce a dissertation or thesis in size than it is to expand it.

As an examiner who has to read 300 pages of thesis in preparation for each *viva*, my eyes need to flow smoothly and easily over the text. Anything that causes me to 'tut' is to be avoided! Unlike fiction or other writing, the reader does not really want to be surprised by the introduction of something unexpected. The inevitable conclusion from this is that writing up all the material requires vast reserves of energy and a remorseless eye for detail. There are some mechanical things that you can adopt to make the process a little less daunting which we will discuss in the next section.

Presentational considerations

One of the maxims of presenting and writing anything, whether it is research or a piece of fiction, is to think of your audience. If you are a research student, your audience is primarily academic since a PhD is concerned about making a contribution to knowledge usually through an empirical study. If you are a taught master's student, your audience is the team of assessors, some of whom may not be familiar with your work. Practically everyone who writes an academic piece of work makes the mistake of not making thoughts and ideas as clear as they should. It is better to aim to oversimplify your work in the first instance than run the risk of making it hard to follow. Your readers will find your ideas more compelling if they can understand them readily. As the researcher and writer, you generally get so involved with your work that all the linkages and assumptions in it are blindingly obvious to you. These linkages and assumptions are not so obvious to your readers or listeners. Therefore, you must tell them in detail how you made every step, why you took that particular step and what the outcome of that step was.

Headings and sub-headings

The use of headings and sub-headings is of great value to you as a writer and to your readers. First, they allow you to break up what can be quite large chunks of writing into manageable sections. Second, these chunks can then be moved around so that the flow of the thesis and the various arguments that you are developing can be strengthened. Your literature review, for example, may be one of the first parts of your thesis that you start to write. As stated in Chapter 3, the literature review is not a summary of what has been written about the theoretical domain of your investigation. The review is a carefully constructed argument or rationale that highlights gaps in the literature, exposes weaknesses in existing research, identifies how research can be expanded upon or proposes alternative methodologies. You will need to subdivide the review into sections of about 800–1000 words so that you can concisely but fully address this particular aspect of the theory that underpins your investigation. Any suggestions of section and paragraph lengths are made very tentatively as it will depend very much on your personal writing style, what you are trying to achieve and how any section fits into the chapter as a whole.

Paragraph and sentence structure

This book is not about how to write English but there are some mistakes that are repeated by students, both native and non-native speakers. The sections that are described above are of course made up of sentences and paragraphs. Sentences should contain just one idea and should follow basic grammatical rules, and should have a subject, finite verb and object. If you are unsure of these, go and read broadsheet newspapers and some good fiction or biography so that you can refresh your understanding of English grammar. Paragraphs should cover an idea or theme with all the sentences in that para-graph relating to that theme. A paragraph should be made up of at least six or seven sentences. A paragraph is not a section and it might be expected that each section would comprise three to five paragraphs. As you become more familiar with the practice of writing and as you read more and more, it will become a little less daunting. All of these suggestions underline the earlier statement about writing up your research from the start of your investigation. As far as reading and writing are concerned, let yourself be inspired by the style of established writers, both academic and non-academic.

Countdown

Master's students usually work to a date when their dissertation needs to be handed in. Supervisors usually observe that students allow too little time to work on their dis-sertation and are constantly trying to come up with ways of encouraging students to start work on their research from the very beginning. Research students usually devote themselves to their study full time but have to submit three years after registering. Either way, it is important to try and plan together with your supervisor key stages and dates in your work as well as those required by the institution. This type of planning helps in two ways. First, it breaks up the time into manageable chunks with outcomes for each chunk. Second, it provides a feeling of achievement when you meet the deadline with the com-pleted piece of work. This unfortunately will not always happen but if you practice meet-ing deadlines you will get better at it. Your supervisor will help you set realistic targets.

Satisfiers and dissatisfiers

There is something of a pedigree to this sub-heading and it must be attributed to Johnston (1995) where it relates to a study into financial services marketing. I adapt this construct to dissertations and theses as a means of illustrating the sort of thing that should and should not appear in a completed dissertation or thesis. The impor-tance of removing or ensuring the total absence of dissatisfiers is to allow the reader to appreciate your research to the full without being distracted by minor mistakes. Satisfiers are those aspects of your research which will please or even delight the reader. The relationship between the two is that one cannot appreciate the satisfiers if dissatisfiers are present (see Table 8.1). In line with Johnston's premise, satisfiers and dissatisfiers are not directly related and as such they are represented quite separately. Satisfiers are elements of your dissertation or thesis which are likely to enhance the reader's impression of your work, such as presentation, signposting and fully labelled and explained figures and tables. Dissatisfiers are those elements which are likely to irritate the reader, such as typos or mistakes on the first few pages (later is not quite so bad), incorrect or inconsistent referencing, misspelling of author names, poor labelling of diagrams. The important thing to remember about satisfiers and dissatisfiers is that satisfiers do **not** cancel out dissatisfiers. The dissatisfiers have been eliminated for the value of the satisfiers to kick in.

Title and abstract

You will have heard the expression that first impressions count and this is just as true in presenting your research as anywhere else. The aim is to have a title that is compelling and relatively concise. You were advised in Chapter 2 to practice telling people about your research in a sentence. During the course of your investigation, you will have refined this sentence. This refined version will form the core of your title, which should convey the dominant theory and the context of the research. It is not very important whether your title takes the form of a question, for example:

What is the impact of customer loyalty on retail staff in SMEs? A case study approach

or a statement such as:

An investigation into accounting practices in immigrant domestic services companies: a case study.

You will note that in these examples, a description of the method has been included. Although this is not essential, some information about the research strategy has to be provided early in the research. Do not forget that confusion persists over case study and case study research, so it is essential that you make it clear to the reader that your research strategy is case study research.

Your dissertation or thesis will be prefaced with an abstract. The length of this abstract will depend on the regulations of your institution but an average length would be 300 words. As always, you are urged to find a good example of an abstract to use as a model for your own abstract. Several publishers of academic journal articles recommend a structured abstract for their authors and Table 8.1 provides an illustration. You do not have to use the headings that are in the left-hand column but you can write your abstract following that structure. It is a very useful exercise and should not be left until the end. It is sadly rather easy to lose sight of the purpose of your research and this is something that the reader is very keen to know right from the beginning.

Table 8.1   Abstract template

Abstract section	Content
Purpose	Tells the reader succinctly what the research sets out to do with concise reference to theory.
Method	Provides overview of approach, strategy, data collection and analysis.
Findings	Summarizes what the data collection/analysis tells us.
Implications	Indicates the relevance of your research to managers, policy makers or practitioners.
Contribution	Provides detail on how the findings take research in the area forward, including suggested areas of further research.

In the process of doing your dissertation or thesis, it is of the highest importance that you constantly keep in mind the purpose of your research, again keeping it as concise and focused in your mind and in describing it to others as you can. It is far too easy to go down blind alleys. Your supervisory team will have kept you on track as much as possible. It is worth referring back to your research question/problem and objectives once a week at least and thinking about the abstract is a good mechanism for focus.

Structure

Your dissertation or thesis will be organized in chapters in due course but you will not necessarily write initially in chapters nor will you write the chapters in the order that they

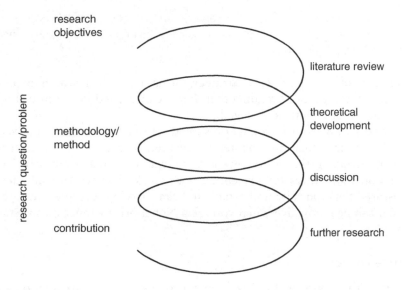

Figure 8.1   Research core

will eventually appear. Most students start with the literature which is clearly needed to frame the research and bound the case. Sometimes, you can have more than one section on the go at the same time. At other times, you will need a change from the literature that you are attempting to grapple with. If you reach this point rather than giving the research a complete rest (and sometimes this has to be done), try to read up on another aspect of your research, for example research methods, which can at least provide a change of scene. Reading about and writing up your methodology and method will absorb some of your intellectual energies! It is a good idea to think of your dissertation or thesis holistically rather than chapter by chapter. You can do this by mapping the structure of your thesis onto the research objectives. The value of mapping your research in this way makes it easier for you to keep on top of the core arguments that you have adopted for your research question and methodology. Everything that you write needs to be closely related to the central theme (core) of your research question/problem.

Figure 8.1 has the research question/problem as the core with the spiral encompassing all the aspects of the dissertation or thesis.

In the following section, a suggested structure for your dissertation or thesis is presented. I have avoided doing this on a chapter basis because there may be more than one chapter per theme but most investigations follow this kind of structure.

Introduction

You will probably write this chapter towards the end of your investigation, when you have a very clear idea of what you have actually done. This may sound strange but research evolves during its execution and you as a researcher develop. At the end of the dissertation or thesis, you will have acquired research skills and a thorough understanding of your case and data that you did not have at the outset. Your introduction will consist of the background to your research in terms of theory and the case(s) that you are investigating. This chapter must include a very clearly articulated rationale for your research – see, for example, the rationale provided by Kärreman and Rylander (2008: 104) for their research:

> Based on an extensive case study of a management consulting firm, this paper explores how the practice of branding contributes to the processes in which meaning in and about the organization is shaped.

This statement contains the research strategy, the nature of the research (exploratory) and the particular aspect of branding that they are interested in. From this opening, reader's expectations are thus managed.

The second part of your introduction should set out the structure and very brief content of your investigation, chapter by chapter. The reader's expectations are managed by including this overview. As a student, it is highly advisable to abide by conventional structures for presenting your work. The reader/examiner wants to be reassured that you fully understand and can carry out accepted research techniques. You can be innovative when you are a Nobel prize winner or an established researcher.

Literature review

In Chapter 2, the argument for developing a solid theoretical foundation for your study was presented. The literature review is one of the three legs that support the tripod of your research. In a PhD thesis, your review may extend to two chapters where you might be bringing together two or more strands of research. In this case you need to be very careful that the synthesized framework of these two streams is presented. Remember that the review forms the jumping off point for your research, therefore the argument that you build from the literature should flow into the methodology/method chapter, in providing a basis for the methodology and method that you have espoused.

It is good practice to capture the key arguments in your review in figures and tables. One particularly worthwhile activity is the construction of a summary table. A summary table in a literature review summarizes in tabular format the work of key contributors to the theory that underpins your investigation, usually presenting the findings, method and research context of each study. A good example of a summary table can be found in Hughes et al. (2010) but find one that suits you and your investigation. All your tables and figures need to be accompanied by a thorough explanation of your figure or table. It is strongly recommended that writers never finish a section or chapter with a figure or table but include a paragraph below showing how it contributes to the arguments that are being developed.

Students often reproduce the figures and tables of published authors as part of their literature reviews. As part of your learning process, it might just be justifiable to do this at the beginning of your study. Once you have mastered the content of the concepts or material therein, you should aim to develop your own or at the very least modify existing work to demonstrate that you have thought beyond the original contribution. Make sure that you attribute the work correctly.

Methodology and method

Students seem to find structuring and presenting this chapter more difficult than other parts of their dissertation or thesis. Business research methods are frequently derived from methods used by the social scientists. Research students, therefore, should aim to base a proportion of their methodology and method on research contributions from social scientists, who have made investigations using a similar research design to that of yours. If you are a research student, this chapter will have a significant section on the epistemological and methodological foundations of your research (see Chapter 2). I would suggest that references for this chapter include social science research books such as Creswell (2007) and de Vaus (2002), business research texts such as Maylor and Blackmon (2005), specialist research books such as Yin (2009) and papers where the research method is appropriate such as Eisenhardt (1989) and Kärreman and Rylander (2008). Case study research is often used in nursing as well, for example Glaser (1966), and you may find it helpful to consult papers outside the business disciplines. Examiners and readers would conclude that the inclusion of sources outside business and management shows that you have read widely and critically.

As far as the structure of the chapter on methodology and methods is concerned, it can usefully begin with a restatement of your research objectives. By restating your objectives at this point, you are reminding the reader of the purpose of the study and you will then find it relatively straightforward to move into the detail of the methodology and method. You do not have to write the methodology and method as one chapter. Some research students may seek to write a chapter on each (as indeed I did) and this is something to discuss with your supervisory team. Whichever structure you choose, there will be an account of the theoretical foundations of your study as well as a detailed description of the steps in the research design. The following extract shows how authors in an analysis of case study research in tourism link two sections of their paper together.

> ... this paper suggests that, to a large extent, the stereotypical perceptions of case study research in tourism are not justified, and therefore such a perspective should be taken critically in the evaluation of tourism research and scholarship.
>
> **2. Case study as a research strategy**
>
> Case studies have long been a topic of interest in the methodological literature. In a historical review of this approach, Platt (1992) observed a rise (in the 1930s) and fall (during World War II) of its earlier use and a revival of interest in this approach since the late 1960s and/or early 1970s.
>
> (Xiao and Smith 2006)

In the first section, the authors comment on unjustified perceptions of case study research in tourism. In the second section, they move on to observing the established position of case study research in methodological literature. What you should be aiming to avoid is any interruption in the reader's progress through your dissertation or thesis. The reader will want to see how each section logically follows on from the preceding one.

A suggested structure for the methodology/method chapter is shown in Table 8.2. Even if you decide to write the material in two chapters, the table provides guidance on what should be included. As stated above, the aim is to ensure that each section follows on from the preceding one and builds a platform for the ensuing section.

The aim of Table 8.2 is to provide a suggested structure for the methodology/ methods chapter so that the researcher can provide a coherent account of the research steps that were taken and the methodology in which they were embedded. Case study research quality may have been undermined in the past by insufficient detail about the data collection, particularly secondary data and the analysis. Readers must have

Table 8.2   Structure of methodology/method chapter

Heading	Typical content
Introduction	Statement of chapter contents, reiteration of research question/problem and objectives, following up on concluding comments of the preceding chapter (literature review), leading into the next section on methodology
Methodology	Philosophical foundations of the study such as interpretivist traditions, implications of methodological stance on method, leading into the research strategy
Research strategy	Case study research, how many cases, embedded, comparative, selection criteria, leading into ethics and access
Ethics and access	What ethical issues arose from the research strategy? How were they addressed? How was access negotiated and led into data collection?
Data collection	Careful explanation and presentation of multiple data sources using diagrams to assist reader understanding. Detail of informant selection, interview guides, focus group prompts, how questionnaire items were developed and measured. Very precise details of secondary data sources and how they were evaluated, leading into analysis
Data analysis and triangulation	Detailed explanation of how each data source analysed, followed by section on triangulation (data)
Research quality/credibility	How the data and findings of research were evaluated according to appropriate (to methodology) criteria
Conclusion	An evaluation or reflection of the methodology/method in the study. Providing a bridge into the following chapter on findings.

the detail that has been mapped out for you in preceding chapters, which supports your arguments for research quality. If the reader has understood all the steps in the research design and seen the evidence of the findings that you have analysed, then they will be more open to your conclusions and the contribution of your research.

Presenting your findings

At the end of your data collection, you will have amassed an enormous amount of data from various sources and possibly in quite different formats. Since you are engaged in case study research, the data and findings could consist of qualitative or quantitative and primary and/or secondary material. The challenge that you face in compiling your first draft is how to present these data so that they support the themes/dimensions that you have identified. As always, look for examples in published articles where similar research has been conducted, not forgetting for one moment about your audience. You should not restrict your search for examples of good presentation practice to case study research. Look at papers in any good quality journals within and beyond your discipline. Your objective is to present the findings of the case or cases which will require you to organize your findings across the data sets. You may find that you do present some of the findings according to their data source initially but you must then move on to link them explicitly with the other data sets. Make sure that these linkages are ultra clear, as it is always easy for a writer to make assumptions that the reader will follow the 'jumps' that are being made. Generally they do not! Remember that the data sources have generated data according to the research strategy that you adopted to address your research question. The challenge for the case study researcher therefore is to present the findings in such a way that all the data sources contribute to the overall research. Presenting data from each data source is probably not going to fulfil this objective, so you should organize your findings under emergent or pre-determined themes/dimensions (see Chapter 6). You will know after your analysis what these dimensions/themes are and they will form the basic structure of the findings chapter. If your research tends towards the deductive and your analysis has consisted of seeking support for your theory, then you may prefer to use sub-headings that are derived from the literature (pre-determined or a priori). If, on the other hand, your research leans towards the inductive, it is quite common for sub-headings to be derived from the findings (often referred to as *in vivo*). This distinction is important as it indicates to the reader that you are being consistent in your research approach. Leave plenty of time for this as it is a process often referred to as iterative which roughly translates into having to do it several times over.

Once the question of sub-headings is understood and put in place, you can then begin to select which data you are going to include under those themes/dimensions that best capture or illustrate how that theme/dimension is supported. Ensure that you use the complete range of data that you have collected, as you have argued in previous chapters the reasons why these data sets contribute to addressing the research question/problem. Each extract from your data set has to be discussed with reference to the relevant literature, so that the reader understands why this particular extract has been selected and how it fits into the investigation. This practice also contributes to analytic generalizability and other quality measures discussed in Chapter 7. The extracts can take a number of forms but again you must explain why you have chosen this particular format on this occasion, label it appropriately and tell the reader how it contributes to the research. Tragically (or so it might appear) from all the data that you have amassed, you will probably use only a very small proportion in your findings section. The way that you collect your data is always more important than the quantity as this contributes more to assessments of quality.

Extracts from interview and focus group are often presented as quotations, for example from this case study into latent organizations in the Dutch film industry:

> When you have a strong relationship, you are more inclined to accept this [budgetary problem]. You understand better and it is easier to accept what the problems are for the producer. You may be able to avoid this next time. (Director E)
>
> (Ebbers and Wijnberg 2009)

In the following research insight and example which follows, Eisenhardt (1989) suggests that summarizing work in tables aids in reader comprehension.

Research insight: super summary

Smart et al. (2009) identified 66 activities under five themes which they had identified for business process management (BPM) and summarized their business process management research in a table (Table 8.3). The researchers adopted a deductive approach, using pre-determined codes that had been decided in advance of the analysis. In this table, the letters in the top line refer to their informants and the activities in the column on the left refer to the five BPM themes. The numbers in each column refer to the total number of activities which each informant allocated to each theme.

Table 8.3   Five BPM themes

	A	B	C	D	E	F	G	
Strategy			2	2	1	1	1	7
Architecture	1	2	2	2	4	3	2	16
Ownership	1	1	2	3	1	3	1	12
Measurement	1	1	3	6	4	1	1	17
Improvement	1	3	2	5	1	1	1	14
Total								66

This is quite an extreme example of reducing data but may be worth considering within the context of your research.

As an alternative to tables, consider the use of figures to illustrate how a major theme relates to its sub-themes. Map out the themes roughly on paper or whiteboard and see if you can make justifiable links or connections across the data sets, themes or dimensions. Adapt existing models such as matrices, flow charts or daisy wheels initially to assist but reject them if they do not support the way that your findings are developing. Discuss these figures with colleagues and your supervisor, making sure that everything is grounded in the data. When you are happy with the model, only then use appropriate software to reproduce it, giving it a title and labelling it in accordance with the system that you are using. It is usual in dissertations or theses to number headings and sub-headings but check with your supervisor and with the regulations of your course. To assist the reader in following the flow of your work, provide links from one sub-headed section to another. Your findings chapter will consist of sections with sub-headings corresponding to dimensions/themes of the research. In each section, you will discuss the findings using extracts presented in a range of formats discussed with reference to the literature. The aim of this chapter is to begin to argue for the contribution of the study based on your findings, hence the close association between literature and data. This chapter, if written as suggested, then allows you to move smoothly on to the discussion.

Discussion

You have now presented your findings accessibly and attractively and you have enfolded them with the literature (Eisenhardt 1989), which means that you have referred back to the literature at each point that you are making. In the discussion chapter, you take a step back from the detail of data that you have included in the findings chapter and evaluate the main themes or dimensions of your research within the conceptual framework of your research. You may find that the study conducted by Ebbers and Wijnberg (2009) generates some good principles for presenting your findings and discussion. You may wish to structure this chapter around the same theme/dimensions that you used in the previous chapter or you may have had some ideas about a higher level of abstraction, again which you will have argued for in the methodology/methods chapter. Whatever you decide, make sure that you inform the reader in the introduction to the chapter, how you are presenting this chapter and why you have chosen to do it this way. Brauer (2009), for example, develops his theoretical framework around a classical 2 by 2 matrix in which he embeds the literature relating to each quadrant. He then returns to this matrix in the results and discussion section, expanding the model with an arrow illustrating two stages in the process of divestiture. The reader can see easily how the initial theoretical framework has been advanced and hence the contribution to knowledge that the research claims. The virtue of this particular example is its simplicity and clarity. Keep your diagrams straightforward and uncomplicated but make sure that they include some advancement or contribution that is evidenced in the findings.

Allow plenty of time for writing the discussion chapter as it is where the intellectual force of your research is demonstrated. You will inevitably have been turning over in your mind the implications of your research findings during the course of the study and, as recommended in the first chapter, you will have been making notes as you progressed. These notes will have captured your thoughts and reflections as you work through the data and will prove immensely valuable at this stage where you will need to demonstrate insight. There will be several individual drafts of this chapter as you will be discussing each element of your findings in relation to the literature that you drew upon in the literature review. It will take some time to get the level of the discussion right (more iterations). Your supervisor(s) will again play a key role here. A well-structured discussion chapter will then allow you to make credible claims about the contribution to knowledge and practice.

Conclusion

You are nearing the end of your investigation and the light at the end of the tunnel has grown considerably brighter but contain your excitement. It seems that you have just the conclusion to write. The error is to think that this is a straightforward task as the conclusion is remarkably time-absorbing and needs to be crafted with considerable care. Three areas to address in your conclusion are discussed below.

Reminding the reader

Your readers will appreciate being reminded at this point what your dissertation or thesis has been about. You should restate your research question or problem for them, highlighting the original gap or extension to the literature that you have chosen to research. Also give a brief overview of your research approach since a case study has implications for a particular type of study.

What you have achieved

At research level, a statement of your contribution to knowledge must be made very explicitly. The aim of making a contribution is something that will have shaped your whole thesis and the statement will form the centrepiece of this chapter. You will have devoted your literature review to identifying the gap or the new work that is required. Adopting a case study approach conveys to the reader that you are investigating your research question in depth and within a particular context. Note the language of published case study researchers in the way that they state their contribution; it is a lesson in measured prose with very careful wording.

If your research is at master's level then a contribution is not required in the same way. Instead, you will have developed your research question from the literature to investigate a particular theoretical framework within a business context. Again, choosing a case study research strategy implies that you are looking at this research question in depth and within a specific context.

You may also want to make a short, modest statement of the limitations of the study. Some students tend to provide quite a long account of the limitations of their research, which is something of an 'own goal'. The readers/examiners will have their own ideas about its limitations, so do not give them too much ammunition. However, you can remind the reader about what case study research can and cannot do, just to pre-empt those rather well-worn criticisms that you will have more than addressed in your dissertation or thesis.

Implications of your research

It is expected in a thesis to see suggestions for further research. You do not want your readers/examiners under-appreciating the benefits of this particular research approach. If you have framed your study according to the research protocols cited in this book, then two to three areas for investigation in the future will have emerged. One of these suggestions could be a wider study such as a survey but state this carefully so that you do not undermine your case study strategy. The suggestions need to be very closely aligned with what you have found.

Since you are looking at a business or management related research problem, you will also need to write about the practical implications of your research for the discipline. As Oliver (2008) states, these implications should not take the form of a list of recommendations. This would not be appropriate in case study research because of the generalization issues attached to this style of research.

Drafts

You *must* begin writing your research at the very beginning of the research process. This maxim cannot be stated too often. Most institutions have stages through which students have to pass *en route* to their qualification. These stages involve the preparation of chapters or summaries of their work for scrutiny by supervisors and other academics with relevant expertise either in the subject or in supervising dissertations or theses. Supervisors usually advise students to write their research up chapter by chapter and provide feedback as each chapter is drafted. This is very common practice and worth sticking to. However, a dissertation or thesis is more than a collection of chapters. It is a closely argued investigation with a strong academic theme running through it. The implications of this statement are that only when all the chapters are completed, can work on the draft thesis really start. This may come as something of a shock as students can often put a great deal of time into polishing each chapter only to be informed that as a whole the thesis needs further work in a number of chapters. To be fair to supervisors, this unwelcome advice will arise only when they can see the overall direction and content of the thesis and appreciate where inconsistencies and gaps lie. The main thing to remember is to allow time for writing two to three drafts of the whole dissertation or thesis in your countdown to submission, even if you and your supervisor are quite pleased with each chapter. The assessors will be looking at the dissertation or thesis as a whole and judging it on its overall coherence and how each chapter contributes to that overall flow.

First draft

For the first draft of your dissertation or thesis, you should aim for each chapter to be written so that it is complete in every way, as follows:

- There are no gaps that remain to be filled.
- All diagrams and figures are thoughtfully presented and labelled clearly and appropriately.
- References are checked are for presentation in the required way and they are all there!

It is no help to your supervisors in gauging the quality and contribution of your dissertation or thesis if there are incomplete sections. Pay attention to margins, headings and spacing with special attention to the regulations of the institution with whom you are studying. Remember the satisfiers and dissatisfiers!

Working with examples

I always recommend to my students that they choose a number of papers and at least one dissertation or thesis to guide their work. You should discuss these examples of good practice with your supervisor to check that they do correspond with their idea of a good example. It is not always straightforward to assess the quality of a piece of work, especially if you are a novice. Even experts may have divergent views about the quality of an academic piece of work. The aim of these models that you have chosen is to demonstrate particular aspects of good practice for example a well-constructed literature review. It is also very useful to have a model of a research design that more or less fits with what you are aiming to do. If this research has been published in a peer-reviewed journal then the steps that the researchers have taken in their research method will have satisfied their reviewers and therefore provide a good template for you. I have used examples of peer-reviewed case studies and other research in the book to illustrate this point. You may think that this is rather limiting but I would advise that you learn the basics of research before you try anything too exciting. Your assessors will want to be reassured that you have understood the basic principles of research methods. Therefore, it is strongly recommended that you make abundantly clear every single step of your research with close reference to the relevant literature.

Using published work as a guide is perfectly acceptable but make sure that you attribute everything that you use to avoid any possible suspicions of cheating. It is also a good idea to look at dissertations or theses and to use them as models to follow or, sadly, in some cases to avoid.

Working with others

You will remember from the introduction that writing your dissertation or thesis requires vast reserves of energy and a remorseless eye for detail.

Your supervisor

Your relationship with your supervisor needs to be one where you respect each other. PhD students usually have quite a close relationship with their supervisor owing to the length of time and the intensity of the study. There are plenty of texts that suggest how you manage your relationship with your supervisor (for example, Oliver 2008). From my perspective as a supervisor, it is helpful if students:

- Submit work regularly and on time.
- Arrange meetings in advance.
- Tell me when they are feeling particularly stressed or have a problem.
- Maintain accurate records of meetings, suggestions and feedback.
- Participate in all the university/school training events for doctoral and master's students.
- Work flat out!

Writing dissertations or theses is an example of independent study where you need to take responsibility for your own progress. A supervisor is there to guide and direct you but not to teach you in the conventional sense.

Your colleagues

Writing a dissertation or thesis, rather like writing a book, can be a rather solitary pursuit and your colleagues at the business school and/or university can be of great solace and support. You are strongly advised to discuss your research informally over coffee/tea and formally in seminars with your colleagues. They can be of very great assistance both emotionally and with research. No one quite understands what doing a PhD is like other than those who have submitted one or are doing one. You may find it helpful to discuss your sufferings. Even more importantly, discussing your work will almost certainly generate some very useful ideas, further reading, presentational practices or methodological/methods clarification. Build a network inside the school, in the university and with doctoral students in other institutions. The cultivation of a group of working colleagues is essential to working effectively unless you are really a very independent person. Business schools recognize this and ensure that research students become part of a community of researchers who can share knowledge, experiences and skills. There will be research seminars where you and your colleagues will present your work to sympathetic audiences, transfer events where students move from MPhil to PhD study, social events where you can meet colleagues in other subject areas such as life sciences and arts, training courses (do not miss on any account!) and informal events. Make sure that you are involved and consider organizing the occasional event yourself. You will have times when it all seems rather too much to cope with and talking to your colleagues will make you appreciate that these feelings are not uncommon and that you are not alone!

Friends and family

Your colleagues will provide lots of encouragement and guidance but you have another resource that you should not overlook and that is your friends and family. You will also have friends outside of the research community and it is important to get out and enjoy yourself and escape from what at times may seem a very heavy burden. Organize your diary so that you have something to look forward to every few days. You will then return refreshed to your studies. This sounds obvious but sometimes you can become very fixed on hitting a deadline without realizing that you need a break. In adjusting to a prolonged and sustained period of study, you may have found that you need to adjust the way that you work. If you have been someone who has always worked to a last-minute model, this is not something that you can replicate successfully for a dissertation or thesis. I have had frank and forthright discussions with my students about the way that they work where they have insisted that they know what they are doing. My counter argument is that the need to complete a research thesis in three years means that preferred ways of working may have to be revisited. Styles of working are something else worth discussing with your supervisor as well as the material/content of your dissertation or thesis.

Putting your research out there (or 'don't be shy')

If you are a research student, then you should present your work at conferences at the very least. Your supervisor will advise you about what aspects of your research you can submit to colloquia and conferences in your discipline. You will also benefit from very experienced tutors at doctoral colloquia who will give you supportive but incisive feedback on your research so far. When you have findings to report then consider preparing a submission to a journal. Writing for an external audience is a very important part of your research development and the benefits extend well beyond the writing of the paper and its presentation. At a research colloquium, you will meet other students who are engaged in similar endeavours and with common experiences. Go and talk to these people about your research.

Presenting your work at a doctoral colloquium will provide you with feedback that should enable you to progress this work into a journal submission. There are a number of benefits in writing a journal paper during the course of your studies. The first benefit is to further perfect the art of presenting your ideas in academic format. Second, in submitting your work for peer review and, in this case, the peers are academics who are acknowledged as experts in the same field as you, you will gain high quality feedback on your work. Third, if you are fortunate enough to have your work published, it sends a signal to you and your readers that your work is making a contribution to the discipline. This acts as a real boost to your confidence and will assist you through the tough times which can accompany prolonged independent study. It would seem that the benefits clearly outweigh the costs but there is a great deal of effort in writing a journal submission, so, again, discuss with your supervisor.

Summary

In this chapter, we have widened our review of case study research methods to include the writing up and presentation of your work. It has been argued, hopefully with conviction, that style is as important as content and that attention to detail in presentation is essential. The following bullet points summarize the key points of the chapter:

- Structure your dissertation or thesis according to recognized formats. Readers to some extent will expect to see a logical and familiar format.
- Make sure that all dissatisfiers are eliminated.
- Your dissertation or thesis consists of a tripod: literature review, research methodology/method and discussion. These three legs of the tripod need to be closely interlinked.
- Use examples of published work to give you ideas of presenting your work, especially your findings, imaginatively. Make sure that all diagrams, figures and tables are fully if not exhaustively explained.

Exercises

1 Study 25 dissertation titles across the business disciplines which are at the same level as your own work, that is master's or research. What do these titles tell the reader about the research? Does it provide enough information about the aim of the research? Does it sound interesting? Is the title clear and unequivocal? What does a longer title tend to suggest about the work?

2 Write an abstract of your work using the template provided. Ask a colleague who knows your work to read the abstract and comment on how effectively it captures your work. Ask a colleague who is not familiar with your work to read the abstract and then tell you what they think your work is about.

3 Study the structure of an academic article that is in your opinion easy to read. Write down five reasons why this paper is easy to read. What can you borrow from the way that this paper is written for your own research?

Key words

Dissatisfiers are those elements in a dissertation or thesis which cause the reader to stop and wonder about the overall quality of the work. They can be apparently quite insignificant but detract disproportionately from the whole. They are faults which no amount of satisfiers will overcome.

Satisfiers are the elements in a dissertation or thesis which convey the quality and potential contribution of the work. They can include careful presentation of data sources, clear and informative figures and tables as well as accessible writing style. They are quite independent of dissatisfiers.

Further reading

Oliver, P. (2008) *Writing Your Thesis*, London: Sage Publications.

References

Brauer, M. (2009) 'Corporate and divisional manager involvement in divestitures – a contingent analysis', *British Journal of Management*, 20, 341–362.

Creswell, J. W. (2007) *Qualitative Enquiry and Research Design: Choosing Among Five Approaches*, Thousand Oaks, CA: Sage Publications.

de Vaus, D. (2002) *Surveys in Social Research*, fifth edition, London: Routledge.

Ebbers, J. and Wijnberg, N. (2009) 'Organizational memory: from expectations memory to procedural memory', *British Journal of Management*, 20, 478–490.

Eisenhardt, K. (1989) 'Building theories from case study research', *Academy of Management Review*, 14, 4, 532–550.

Glaser, B. (1966) 'The purpose and credibility of qualitative research', *Nursing Research*, 15, 1, 56–61.

Hughes, M., Hughes, P., Mellahi, K. and Guermat, C. (2010) 'Short-term versus long-term impact of managers: evidence from the football industry', *British Journal of Management*, 21, 571–589.

Johnston, R. (1995) 'The determinants of service quality: satisfiers and dissatisfiers', *International Journal of Service Industry Management*, 6, 5, 53–71.

Kärreman, D. and Rylander, A. (2008) 'Managing meaning through branding: the case of a consulting firm', *Organization Studies*, 29, 103–125.

Maylor, H. and Blackmon, K. (2005) *Researching Business and Management*, Basingstoke: Palgrave Macmillan.

Oliver, P. (2008) *Writing Your Thesis*, London: Sage Publications.

Platt, J. (1992) '"Case study" in American methodological thought', *Current Sociology*, 40, 17–48.

Smart, P., Maddern, H. and Maull, R. (2009) Understanding business process management: implications for theory and practice, *British Journal of Management*, 20, 4, 491–507.

Xiao, H. and Smith, S. (2006) 'Case studies in tourism research: a state-of-the-art analysis', *Tourism Management*, 27, 738–749.

Yin, R. (2009) *Case Study Research: Design and Methods*, fourth edition, Thousand Oaks, CA: Sage Publications.

Index

Page references to Figures or Tables will be in *italics*